RUDOLF STEINER (1861–1925) called his spiritual philosophy 'anthroposophy', meaning 'wisdom of the human being'. As a highly developed seer, he based his work on direct knowledge and perception of spiritual dimensions. He initiated a modern and universal 'science of spirit', accessible to anyone willing to exercise clear and unprejudiced thinking.

From his spiritual investigations Steiner provided suggestions for the renewal of many activities, including education (both general and special), agriculture, medicine, economics, architecture, science, philosophy, religion and the arts. Today there are thousands of schools, clinics, farms and other organizations involved in practical work based on his principles. His many published works feature his research into the spiritual nature of the human being, the evolution of the world and humanity, and methods of personal development. Steiner wrote some 30 books and delivered over 6000 lectures across Europe. In 1924 he founded the General Anthroposophical Society, which today has branches throughout the world.

Into human souls I'll guide
sense of spirit, to willingly
waken in hearts the Easter word;

with human spirits I will think
warmth of soul, that powerfully
they may feel the risen one;

brightly in death's apparent face
shines spirit understanding's earthly flame;
and self becomes the eye and ear of worlds.

EASTER

Festivals

Also available:

RUDOLF STEINER

EASTER
An Introductory Reader

Compiled with an introduction, commentary and notes by Matthew Barton

Sophia Books

Sophia Books
An imprint of Rudolf Steiner Press
Hillside House, The Square
Forest Row, RH18 5ES

www.rudolfsteinerpress.com

Published by Rudolf Steiner Press 2007

For earlier English publications of individual selections please
see pp. 147–8

The material by Rudolf Steiner was originally published in
German in various volumes of the 'GA' (*Rudolf Steiner
Gesamtausgabe* or Collected Works) by Rudolf Steiner Verlag,
Dornach. This authorized volume is published by permission of
the Rudolf Steiner Nachlassverwaltung, Dornach (for further
information see pp. 151–2)

All translations revised by Matthew Barton

*Matthew Barton would like to thank Margaret Jonas, librarian at Rudolf
Steiner House, for her invaluable help in locating volumes used in
compiling this book.*

A catalogue record for this book is available from the British
Library

ISBN 978 185584 139 0

Cover by Andrew Morgan
Typeset by DP Photosetting, Neath, West Glamorgan
Printed by Cromwell Press Ltd., Trowbridge, Wiltshire

Contents

GOLGOTHA, THE CENTRAL DEED OF EVOLUTION

EASTER, A FESTIVAL FOR THE FUTURE

Introduction

In George Herbert's poem 'Easter Wings', written during the second half of the seventeenth century, he arranges words on the page in the shape of contracting and then expanding patterns. Here is the first verse:

LORD, who createdst man in wealth and store,
Though foolishly he lost the same,
Decaying more and more,
Till he became
Most poor:

With thee
O let me rise
As larks, harmoniously,
And sing this day thy victories:
Then shall the fall further the flight in me.

As one can see, the words reflect this narrowing and enlarging dynamic, so that form and content are perfectly matched; and at the point where the first direction changes to the second, resolving one, is a space. This is an extremely active space, I would say, the place where the radical change in direction occurs.

It may not be too far-fetched, either, to find in the rhyme words a tighter, narrower feeling in the first part of the verse and a widening, rising feeling in the second, taking flight finally in the winging 'f' sounds of the last line. One could also perhaps imagine the pattern, looking down on it from above, as a descending and then rising slope, the space between the two halves forming the deepest part of a valley. In the poem, of course, what is imagined but left unuttered in the space between the two halves — perhaps because it is unutterable — is the event at Golgotha which we celebrate at Easter.

In terms of individual experience one might also see this space as a void in the soul, the place of emptiness but also receptivity we can reach when our powers have failed us, when, for whatever reason, we have reached rock bottom. An empty space, whether of the soul or of a physical kind, can act as a vacuum, drawing in forces that did not previously exist there. A process that continues in us all the time illustrates this rather well, that of breathing. Once we have breathed out all the air within us, our lungs naturally open to receive a new influx, a new impetus. Transferred to the non-material realm, the same process gives us a picture of *inspiration*, a word which of course relates both to the breath and the spirit.

In these lecture extracts, Steiner interweaves many strands of human experience to show that what he calls the Mystery of Golgotha was the radical influx into human life and evolution of an impetus that is, at the same time, both unique and all-pervasive. He places Easter into a multitude of interpenetrating contexts: from the whole sweep of human evolution, through the breathing rhythm of each year's changing seasons, to the free choice of every individual — which one might call 'poise' — in establishing a balance in their lives and outlook between matter and spirit.

It would be a simple step to superimpose on George Herbert's word pattern a lemniscate or figure of eight, which, if we imagine it in movement, has a wonderfully dynamic and continuous quality, embodied for instance in the human circulation, the interpenetration of oxygen and blood. It is surely no accident that the space in the first pattern corresponds to the crossing point of the second, and indeed one can get a sense that this crossing point of the lemniscate is a moment of 'space' between contraction and expansion, the place where the onward impetus is renewed. In the human circulation, of course, this place is occupied by the heart, which lives between the expansion and contraction of systole and diastole, but at the same time forms an organ of mediation and balance between different influences, both in a physical and a non-physical sense. In terms of the year's breathing rhythm, as Steiner describes it, two festivals occupy this crossing point: Easter in spring, and the autumn festival of Michaelmas. The first is the gateway into physical growth, flourishing and fertility, while the second is a door into nature's decay and winter's dark. Steiner has much to say about the relationship between these two festivals, which in different ways both celebrate resurrection.

The themes of many of these extracts range far and wide, but always and inevitably return to that unutterable, silent, dynamic space which Steiner sees as the source of all hope for humanity, as the omnipresent heart of our evolution. The Cross, he says, raises us from death only because it is so firmly planted in it, because a vast, living, non-physical power descended to the very deepest reach of material existence and illumined the darkest recesses of earthly experience. The 'place of the skull' (Golgotha) is an apt name in many ways. The brain inside the skull is of course the least living part of us, with least powers of regeneration and, as Steiner frequently observes, brain-bound thinking is at risk of regarding material existence as the source of everything and sole reality. It might not be too fanciful to see the head and skull as the winter-end of the seasonal cycle, while the metabolic system, with its combustible heat, reflects midsummer. Between these two poles of course lies, again, the rhythmic mediation of the heart. The victory of the physical sun at the spring equinox is a living image of the spirit's ascendency at Easter Sunday, of the new impetus for evolving life.

I may be at risk of trying to connect too many disparate strands, but it strikes me that the Cross of Golgotha, as the symbol of the physical body, and thus of the human experience of death, can be placed within the enlivening, dynamic lemniscate of circulation, and this in turn can be placed into yet another pattern: the spiral or vortex. Only this morning I was out in my garden engaged in what my neighbour might have supposed was either lunacy or sorcery: stirring a 'biodynamic' preparation (for enhanced soil fertility) in a bucket. To mix this preparation fully you stir it vigorously in water, in a circular motion, first one way and then the other, creating a spiral pattern. Once a deep vortex has formed, so that the bottom of the bucket becomes visible, you stir the mixture in the other direction, repeating this alternating process for an hour. Many researchers, such as Schauberger and Schwenk, have observed that water has a continual tendency to form spirals, and that this form is ubiquitous in nature, in everything from clouds to snail-shells—it is, in other words, characteristic of life. It can have both a centrifugal and centripetal direction, that is, either inwards and downwards or outwards and upwards. At the point where the deepest vortex was formed in my bucket and I reversed the direction, chaos was created — an apparently arrythmic turmoil. Superimposing these three different forms on each other, of spiral, lemniscate and cross, they all share a central 'moment' or transition point. In the case of the cross this point has the still fixity of death, in the lemniscate it has the quality of onward dynamic, and in the spiral it has a pulsing commotion as the direction is reversed. If, as it were, one looks 'down' through these three levels — spiral, lemniscate and cross — one can have a sense of Christ's journey, as Steiner describes it, in descending from the cosmos, through the tumult of human passions which he harmonized, the living forces of the earth and the human body which he renewed, and the death of the skull and mineral fixity whose depths he plumbed, illumined and overcame. Only through this descent through all the levels, homing in on the still point of death, could he in turn prefigure humanity's upward, expanding path of ascent. Easter, says Steiner, not only commemorates a past event but heralds a vital future.

The passages and extracts collected here are just that — longer or shorter extracts from the larger context of whole lectures. Steiner developed his lectures into an art form in the best sense, and the reader is referred to the original, complete lectures for the 'total experience' and context from which these passages are drawn.

Matthew Barton

CAN WE CELEBRATE EASTER?

1. Easter in a Time of Catastrophe

Extract from a lecture given in Dornach on
2 April 1920

*Steiner here pinpoints the impossibility of celebrating
Easter today without, at the same time, wresting ourselves free from a materialistic outlook which is completely at odds with its essence and significance.*

Again and again we must ask what a festival such
as Easter means for most of humanity. The thinking
of very large numbers of people who gather
together to celebrate Easter runs along old lines.
They use the old words and go on uttering them
more or less automatically. They make the same
renunciations in the same formulae to which they
have long been accustomed. But do we have any
right today to utter such renunciations when we
observe all around us a distinct unwillingness to
take part in the great changes that are so necessary
in our time? Are we justified in using the words of
Paul, 'Not I, but Christ in me', when we show so
little inclination to examine what it is that has

brought such unhappiness to humanity in the modern age? Should it not be an essential part of the Easter festival that we set out to gain a clear idea of what has befallen humanity, and a clear idea of the fact that only spiritual or supersensible knowledge can lead us out of catastrophe? If the Easter festival, whose whole significance depends on super-sensible knowledge—for sense-based knowledge can never explain the resurrection of Christ Jesus—is to be taken seriously, it must surely be essential to consider how the human faculty of knowledge can once again be imbued with a supersensible char-acter. Should it not dawn on us that all the decep-tion and illusion that pervades modern culture is due to the fact that we no longer take our own sacred festivals seriously?

We keep Easter, the festival of resurrection, but in our materialistic outlook we have long ceased to care whether or not we have any real under-standing of the resurrection ... it is a jest to keep the festival of resurrection and at the same time put our whole faith in modern science, which obviously can never endorse such a resurrection. Materialism and the celebration of Easter are two things that simply cannot exist side by side ...

The only possible way for modern people to have a right feeling for Easter is when they direct their thoughts to the catastrophe in which the world today is plunged. I do not just mean the catastrophe of the recent years of war, but the universal catastrophe in which human beings have lost all idea of the connection between earthly things and what lies beyond the earth. The time has come when we must realize with full and clear consciousness that supersensible knowledge needs to arise from the grave of our materialistic outlook. For together with supersensible knowledge will arise knowledge of Christ Jesus. In fact the only fitting symbol for the Easter festival is that the entire soul destiny of humanity has been crucified on the cross of materialism. But humanity itself must do something before there can arise from the grave of human materialism all that can come from spiritual insight.

Striving for supersensible knowledge is itself an Easter deed, is something which gives us the right to keep Easter once more. Look up to the full moon and feel how it is connected with the human being, and how the reflection of the sun is connected with the moon; then ponder the need today to go in search of a true self-knowledge that allows us to reflect supersensible realities. If we know ourselves to be a reflection of the supersensible, if we grasp how it forms and constitutes us, then we will also find our way back to it. Fundamentally it is arrogance and pride that come to expression in materialistic views of the world ... we do not want to be a reflection of the divine and spiritual, but merely to be the highest of the animals ...

Above all we should remember that although we still have the tradition of an Easter festival celebrated on the first Sunday after the first full moon of spring, yet we have no right to celebrate this if we cling to modern materialistic culture. How can we acquire this right again? We must take the thought of Christ Jesus lying in the grave; of Christ Jesus who at Easter vanquishes the stone that has been rolled over his grave—we must take this thought and unite it with what our soul should feel about purely external, mechanistic science, that it is like a tombstone rolled upon us whose pressure we must exert ourselves to overcome. Then our confession of faith, instead of being merely, 'Not I, but the fully developed animal in me,' will be, rather, 'Not I, but Christ in me.'

2. Looking Beyond the Ties of Blood

Extract from a lecture given in Dornach on
3 April 1920

*If Christ is to 'rise' — not once but repeatedly within us —
we need to face and outface two tendencies in ourselves
which are also so evident in the wider world and its
conflicts: nationalism and all insular, exclusive
relationships based on ties of blood; and cold, abstract
thinking, which tries to manipulate social conditions
externally rather than through insight gained from heart-
warmed thoughts.*

To prepare ourselves for the new attitudes of soul
which are needed we can, by looking back, develop a
feeling for the powerful way in which individuals like
Paul brought something quite new into earth evolution at the turning point of history. At the present
time, certainly, such impulses glimmer on, but are
concealed as though under a mound of ashes...

When Paul appeared with his interpretation of
Christianity there was a fundamental break with
the principle of human knowledge determined by

blood ties—the principle that had prevailed, and necessarily so, in former times. Paul was the first to declare that neither blood nor identity of race, nor any factor by which human knowledge had been determined in pre-Christian times could continue to be upheld, but that the human being must now establish his relation to knowledge through inner initiative; that there must be a community of those whom he designated Christians, a community to which people would ally themselves in spirit and soul rather than being placed into it through natural blood connections—one, in other words, which they *chose* to belong to . . . The bond between people in this community of Christians was not to be dependent on the blood, for the blood as vitalizer and sustainer of all that ends with death could provide no assurance of immortality—although in ancient times the spirit and soul shone through it. The spirit and soul needed to be revealed in its essence and purity if the possibility of understanding the problem of death in a non-materialistic way was not to be lost . . .

Christianity summons us not to rely on what is brought into earthly existence at birth but to undergo a transformation, to allow the soul to develop, to be reborn in Christ, to acquire through effort and education, through life itself, what is not acquired through the mere fact of birth . . .

Two of the most unchristian impulses of all took effect in the nineteenth century. The first which came to the fore and gained an even stronger hold over people's minds and emotions was that of nationalism. Here we see the shadow of the old blood principle. The Christian impulse towards universal humanity was completely overshadowed by the principle of nationalism ... The one and only reality befitting the present age would be to overcome and eradicate nationalism, and for people to be stirred by the impulse of the universally human.

The second phenomenon [is to be found] in Bolshevism, which owes its destructive power to the fact that it is a product of the brain pure and simple, of the material brain. I have often described how the material brain really represents a process of decay; materialistic thinking unfolds only through processes of destruction, death processes taking place in the brain. If this kind of thinking is applied, as in Leninism and Trotskyism, to the social order, a destructive process is inevitably set in motion, for such ideas issue from what is itself the foundation of destruction, the ahrimanic principle.[1]

... Nationalism and Leninism are the shovels with which the grave of Christianity is being dug today ... We can here discern a mood that is, in a real sense, the mood of Easter Saturday. Christianity lies in the grave, over which human beings roll a stone, in fact two stones, those of nationalism and externally overlaid socialism. Humanity now needs to inaugurate the time of Easter Sunday, when the stone or stones are rolled away. Christianity will not rise from the grave until human beings overcome nationalistic passions and false forms of socialism; until they learn how to find, out of themselves, the forces that can lead to an understanding of the Mystery of Golgotha.

When, with the mood of soul that prevails in our modern age people profess belief in Christ, the angel can only give the same answer as was given in the days of the Mystery itself: 'He whom ye seek is not here.' At that time he was no longer there because human beings first had to find their way through tradition and scripture before reaching knowledge of their own about the Mystery of Golgotha.[2] Today neither scripture nor tradition tell us those things that need to be known; direct knowledge alone can reveal them. We must work to bring about a time when the angel can answer: 'He whom ye seek is here indeed!' But that will not be until the antichristian impulses of our time are overcome ...

Unconscious hatred of the spirit confronts us in nationalism as well as in erroneous socialism. For think what this hatred of the spirit means today, what nationalism means today! In ancient times nationalism had its good purpose, because knowledge of the spirit was connected with the blood. But to be swayed by nationalistic passions as people are swayed today is completely senseless, because blood relationship is no longer a factor of any real significance. The factor of blood relationship as expressed in nationalism is a pure fiction, an illusion.

For this reason, people who cling to such ideas have no right to celebrate an Easter festival. To celebrate an Easter festival is a lie for them. The truth would consist in the angel again being able to say, or rather say for the first time, 'He whom ye seek is here indeed!' But we can be sure that his presence will only be vouchsafed where the principle of the universally human comes into its own...

The grave will remain covered until people again acquire a true knowledge of the spirit and, through this knowledge, an understanding of universal Christianity. Until then there can be no true Easter festival; until then the black of mourning cannot with integrity be replaced by the dawn red of Easter, for until then this replacement is a human lie. Humanity must seek the spirit — that alone can give meaning to our lives in the modern age.

Those who understand humanity's evolution up until our own times will also understand the words 'My kingdom is not of this world'. If the future is to be one of hope, we must strive for what cannot be 'of this world'. But that of course runs counter to human beings' love of ease. It is easier to set up old traditions as ideals and then to bask in the glow of self-congratulation. This is far pleasanter than to say: 'The great responsibility for the future must be shouldered, and this can be done only if the striving for knowledge of the spirit becomes a driving force in humanity.'

Therefore in our present times Easter must remain a festival of warning rather than of joy. And those whose concern for humanity is deep and true will not use the Easter words 'Christ is risen', but rather 'Christ will and must arise!'

3. Tuning to the Cosmos

Extract from a lecture given in Christiana (Oslo) on
21 May 1923

*Human beings so easily settle into fixed systems that are
at odds with a living, fluctuating, dynamic rhythm.
Steiner urges us here to open our outlook to embrace the
greater wisdom of the cosmos.*

In ancient times, before the Mystery of Golgotha,
the human being stood much closer than we do to
outward nature, to the external world. This state-
ment runs counter to modern beliefs that our
science puts us in an intimate relationship with
nature. It does not in the least. We develop intellectual thoughts about nature drawn only from
external observation, but we no longer experience
and accompany nature inwardly.

Had the human being remained dependent on
and interwoven with the spiritual element in
nature, he would not have become the free being
into which he has been developing during recent
stages of historical evolution. He could not have
attained full ego consciousness ...

Today we have no immediate experience of the fact that we breathe in and out, that the air is alternately within us and outside us. Today, unless science informed us of this we would hardly be aware of it, for we do not experience the process of inhaling and exhaling as intimately and vividly as people of ancient times did.

Yet it is not just the human being who breathes but the earth too, although in a somewhat different way.[3] Like us, the earth possesses a soul element, and in the course of a year the earth first breathes in and then breathes out this soul element ...

The Easter festival is set for the first Sunday after the vernal full moon, and thus takes place in conformity with a cosmic dynamic. The reason for this must be sought in ancient times when people experienced how the human soul strives to follow the earth soul on her outward journey to the stars and the cosmos, and seeks guidance from the cosmic wisdom at work there.

Thus the spring festival, the Easter festival, was set not according to earthly but heavenly calculations relating to the cosmos.

Especially during the period between the eighth century BC and the fourth century AD, a sense of sadness prevailed in the souls of people in many civilizations that they could no longer fulfil their longing to follow the earth soul and soar up to the stars in springtime. The human soul, increasingly immersed in the physical body, could no longer do this ... They could therefore easily comprehend why the Easter festival, celebrating Christ's death and resurrection, should occur at this very point during spring ...

The way the date of the Easter festival was set contains profound wisdom. Yet our modern age regards it differently. About 24 years ago I held weekly meetings with a well-known astronomer in a small circle of friends. He could only reason like this: all the account books are thrown into disorder because the Easter festival takes place on different days each year. He believed that, at the very least, it should be set on the first Sunday in April, or regulated in a similar abstract way ...

These things are an outward manifestation of the fact that people want to banish from the world all that obeys dynamic spiritual laws ...

In the spring we can have a vital, vivid experience of the budding and sprouting of young plants, the emergence of flowers, the greening of the trees—in brief, the enlivening of all nature. Likewise we can feel an enlivening of our physical body. After passing through midsummer and coming to autumn we can then feel how nature dies in its outer physical aspect as leaves turn brown, plants wither and fruits are collected and preserved by drying. Something can happen if we experience all this and at the same time have a clear sense of how, as nature is 'carried to the grave', the spiritual sprouts and flourishes ... Something can happen if we experience — with the same solemnly festive mood with which we experience death, entombment and resurrection at Easter — the resurrection of the soul as nature dies back ... We need a connection between the human being and the cosmos. Just as we have the rising and the setting sun, so the death and resurrection of Easter needs to be complemented by the autumn resurrection and death — the resurrection of the human being from dying nature. [We need to] understand how to add to the Easter festival — the festival of rising — the Michael festival at the end of September as the festival of setting ...[4]

THE EARTH AND THE COSMOS

4. The Breathing Earth

Extract from a lecture given in Dornach on
31 March 1923

*Steiner was far in advance of his age in prefiguring James
Lovelock's concept of 'Gaia', of the earth as an ensouled,
living being. He identifies a breathing rhythm in the
succession of the seasons, and says that this rhythm is one
we inevitably accompany and can become conscious of.
Drawing on the image of the lemniscate, or figure of eight,
Steiner places Easter time into a wider rhythm and
context as the gateway into physical growth, with its
reflection in the other gateway, at Michaelmas, of physical decay and spiritual ascent. Michaelmas thus appears
as the deeper meaning of Easter (elsewhere Steiner refers
to it as Easter's 'blossom' and fulfilment).*

Now let us follow the earth further in its yearly
course. Let us follow it up to the time in which we
are just now, about the time of the spring equinox,
the end of March. Then we shall have to imagine
that the earth has just begun to breathe out. The
earth's soul is still half within it, but the earth is

breathing it out: streaming soul forces are pouring out into the cosmos. Whereas since December the forces of the Christ impulse were intimately bound up with the earth, with the soul element of the earth, we now find that this Christ impulse, borne on the outward-streaming soul element, is beginning to radiate around the earth. What is here flowing out into spiritual cosmic breadths of space as Christ-permeated earth soul now necessarily encounters the force of sunlight. We can picture it like this: whereas in December the Christ withdrew the earth soul element into the interior of the earth, insulating it from cosmic influences like a held breath, now, as the earth begins to breathe out, he extends his forces to receive the sun quality which radiates towards him. So we have to depict the sun force and quality uniting with the Christ force radiating from the earth. At Easter, when the earth is breathing out, the Christ begins to work with the sun forces. And what occurs then must not be related to the moon's reflected light, but to the sun directly.

This is the reason why the date of Easter was fixed as the first *Sunday* after the full moon following the spring equinox ...

Easter is on the first Sunday after the spring full moon. Flowing with the earth's outgoing breath the human being rises up with his own being of soul into the cosmic world, permeates and saturates himself with the quality of the stars, takes in the breath of the cosmos with his earthly breath, thus allowing the Easter spirit to penetrate him, and by St John's Day[5] he is most strongly imbued with what he started to be permeated with at Easter. His soul being must then return to the earth as the earth soul is inhaled again, but he depends here on Michael[6] standing beside him so that he may penetrate the earthly world in the right way after the ahrimanic[7] element has been overcome through the forces of Michael.

And ever more and more, as the earth draws in its breath, does the earth's soul element retire into the earth itself up to the time of Christmas.[8] And today we celebrate Christmas time in the right way if we say to ourselves: 'Michael has purified the earth so that the birth of the Christ impulse can occur in the right way at Christmas.'

Then the outflowing into the cosmos begins again. In this outflowing, Christ takes Michael with him so that Michael may again gather to himself out of the cosmos those forces which he has used up in his struggle with the earthly, ahrimanic forces. At Easter time Michael again begins to immerse himself in the cosmos, and is most strongly interwoven with it at St John's.

And today we best understand what unites us as

human beings with the earth if we realize that the Christ impulse is accompanied by Michael throughout the year's course; that, as the Christ force draws down into the earthly and rises up again into the cosmos, it is accompanied by Michael, whose combative activity is at one time focused on the earth, at another is gathering strength for his earthly battle from cosmic breadths of space.

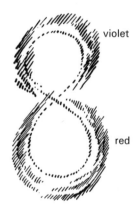

violet

red

In the Easter thought we have an image of utmost grandeur, implanted into earthly conditions to help enlighten us: the image of Christ arising out of the grave in victory over death. We can only grasp this Easter thought in the right way in our time if we complement it with the picture and being of Michael, at the right hand of Christ ...

5. The Year's Rhythmic Cycle: Merging and Sundering

Extract from a lecture given in Dornach on
2 April 1923

*Pursuing the idea of Michaelmas as Easter's fulfilment,
and of the year as a differentiated totality, Steiner here
distinguishes the two qualities we meet in spring and
autumn, and the rhythm flowing between them: a
merging of spirit and body in spring when nature
flourishes, and their separation in autumn when it fades
and dies away. This cyclical dynamic is also one that can
be found in many other spheres. By living into the seasons
we can experience an archetypal rhythm in human life
and experience.*

The spring tends to weave everything together, to
blend everything into a vague, undifferentiated
unity ... The Easter thought loses nothing of value
if the Michaelmas thought is added to it. On the one
hand we have the Easter thought where everything
appears, I might say, as a pantheistic mixture, a
unity ...

Think of this cyclical sequence: first a joining together, intermingling and unifying; then an intermediate state as differentiation takes place; then complete separation, distinction and differentiation; and then once again the merging of what was differentiated within a single whole. In this sequence you always see, besides the two opposite conditions, a third: the rhythm between the differentiated and undifferentiated states ... a rhythm between spirit and matter; their interpenetration followed by their separation ... When, by complementing the Easter thought with the Michael thought in this way we have become able to perceive rightly the primordial trinity in all existence, then we shall absorb this into our whole attitude of soul. Then we shall be able to understand that all life, in fact, depends on the activity and interworking of primordial trinities ...

If we follow the whole course of the year and see how ... spiritual and physical, material life are present as a duality, and how the rhythmic interweaving of these two forms a third element, then we can perceive the three-in-one and one-in-three, and learn to see how the human being can place himself into this cosmic rhythm ...

Then what we need will be present in life: not abstract spirit on the one hand and spirit-void nature on the other, but nature permeated with

spirit, and spirit shaping and forming nature ...
Then the anthroposophical[9] impulse would consist
in perceiving in the Easter season the unity of
science, religion and art; and then at Michaelmas
perceiving how the three—which have a single
mother, the Easter mother—become 'sisters' and
stand side by side, distinct but mutually complementing each other.

6. Spring and Autumn

Extract from a lecture given in Dornach on
21 April 1924

*In these two passages Steiner tells us that festivals of
resurrection used to be celebrated in the autumn and were
only transferred to the physical rebirth of spring when a
sense for the spirit was lost, together with a sense of the
reality of resurrection from death. This is a sense we
urgently need to regain today.*

Thus we look back to a time when certain mysteries
recognized our descent from pre-earthly into earthly
life, while others, the autumnal mysteries, recognized our ascent into the spiritual. In later times,
however, when people no longer sensed this living
relationship between themselves and the cosmos, the
autumnal mystery of ascent was mistakenly combined with the spring mystery of descent into life ...

Through the spring mysteries ... people were
reminded not of how we proceed into the spiritual
world at death, but rather of how we emerge from it
and descend to earth. In other words, precisely

when nature was waxing and sprouting, human beings were reminded of their descent into physical life, while when nature fell into decay they reflected on their rise or resurrection into the spiritual ...

Thus as you can see, Easter as we know it today is encumbered with things that do not really belong to it. It should actually be a ceremony of involvement with the earth, of burial, one that goads us into working, just as the spring festivals did for ancient peoples. Such festivals gave them the spiritual incentives they needed for work in the summer; in other words Easter was an admonishment to prepare for the summer's toil. By contrast the autumn festival of resurrection was celebrated at a time when human beings left work behind. In leaving it behind, however, they experienced within themselves something of supreme importance to beings of spirit and soul—an awakening of the eternal within them. This they experienced by contemplating the soul's resurrection in the spiritual world three days after death ...

Extract from a lecture given in Dornach on 19 April 1924

Human beings had less and less insight into spiritual realities during the centuries that followed [the

Mystery of Golgotha], so that its substance could no longer gain a foothold in their souls. Evolution tended towards the development of a sense for material reality. Human beings could no longer grasp in their hearts that precisely where nature presents itself as ephemeral, as dying and desolate, the spirit's vitality can best be witnessed. The autumnal festival thus lost its meaning. It was no longer understood that the best time to appreciate the resurrection of the human spirit was when outer nature was dying, that is during autumn.

Autumn simply became an unsuitable time for the festival of resurrection for it could no longer turn people's minds to spiritual immortality by underscoring nature's transience. People began to depend on material symbols, upon enduring elements of nature, for their understanding of immortal things. They focused upon the seed's germinating force which, though buried in the autumn, sprouts again in spring. People adopted material symbols for spiritual things because matter could no longer stimulate them to perceive the spirit's reality. Human souls lacked the strength to receive autumn's revelation of the spirit's permanence in contrast to the impermanence of nature. Help from nature in the form of an outwardly visible resurrection was now necessary ...

The need to look to nature for symbols of the

spirit has continued in our own time. Nature, however, provides no complete image of our destiny in death; and while the idea of death has survived, that of resurrection has increasingly disappeared ...

It is anthroposophy's[10] task to add to the thought of death that of resurrection, to inwardly celebrate the resurrection of the human soul and to imbue our whole outlook with an Easter mood ...

7. Necessity and Freedom

Extract from a lecture given in Dornach on
20 April 1924

*Sun and moon, both of which we turn to when deter-
mining the date of Easter each year, have contrasting
qualities that play strongly into our lives: the moon
represents all physical endowments we receive at birth
while the sun, in its spiritual aspect, frees us from compulsion and necessity.*

While the moon forces determine the human being,
permeate us with an inner necessity so that we must
act according to our instincts, our temperament, our
emotions — in a word our whole physical and
etheric nature — the spiritual sun forces free us from
this. They dissolve, so to speak, the forces of compulsion, and it is really through their agency that
we become free.

In ancient times the influence of the moon and
that of the sun were sharply divided. Around the
age of 30 people simply became sun people — that is,
free — whereas up until then they had been moon

people, or unfree. Nowadays these two overlap; even in childhood sun forces act alongside moon forces, and the moon forces continue to work on us in later years. Thus in our time necessity and freedom intermingle ...

Thus we can look back to an ancient time when people spoke of their lunar birth as of a creation by the Father. Regarding their solar birth people understood that in the sun's spiritual rays Christ's power, the power of the Son, is active, and that it sets human beings free. Consider what it does for us. Only through its action can we make something of ourselves in earthly life. Without the liberating forces and impulses of the sun we would be strictly predestined, at the mercy of an inexorable determinism, and not even the determinism of fate, but that of nature ...

For the most part, however, human beings lost this knowledge of the sun. Although knowledge of our dependence on the moon or Father forces remained with people for a long time, awareness of our dependence on sun forces — or we should really say, of our emancipation through these forces — disappeared much earlier. And what today we call the forces of nature, which seem to be the sole topic in modern philosophy, are really nothing but a completely abstract version of the moon forces ...

[In the ancient mysteries] initiates grasped how

sun and moon, as celestial opposites, worked within them. They knew that their physical form, the particular shape of eyes, nose, indeed the entire body, and the fact that this form could grow, were a result of moon forces, and that all necessity depended on these. But the fact that they could come to life within their physical body as free human beings, that they could alter their character and master themselves, was due to the forces of the sun, the Christ forces . . .

From all this one can understand why even today human beings calculate the date of Easter from a particular constellation of sun and moon . . . That Easter is set on the first Sunday following the first full moon after the spring equinox shows . . . that we have retained a sense that Easter must be determined from above, from the cosmos.

8. Moon Versus Sun

Extract from a lecture given in The Hague on
23 March 1913

*The earth, the site of our long evolution, is in a very slow
process of decline. Particularly in our own time of global
warming we can wonder whether our old mother will last
long enough to allow us to complete the evolutionary
development that she sustains.*

*At the Easter when this lecture was given, the equinox,
the first full moon of spring and Easter fell in unusually
close proximity. Steiner here describes the opposition
between moon and sun as the two poles of flourishing and
waning physical life, with their fulfilment and redemption in Christ, the spiritual sun.*

When spring begins, when the sun moves into a
relationship with the earth that enables plant beings
symbolizing all we once possessed in paradise to
burst forth anew from the earth mother through the
sun's power, when the sun relates to the earth in
such a way that the seeds of the plants can germi-
nate and bud, then the human soul begins inwardly

to raise a song of joy, realizing that forces are astir throughout the cosmos which every year, in cyclic succession, conjure forth from the womb of the earth what is necessary for outward life and for the life of the soul—so that we may complete our journey from the beginning to the end of earthly evolution. When the mantle of winter covers the body of the earth, its impressions waken in us the thought of what will one day bring the earth's destruction, rendering it unfit to be our dwelling place. If winter evokes this thought in the human soul, each new spring evokes this other thought: 'O earth, from primal beginnings you are endowed with perpetually new forces of youth, with ever-renewing life; you have the power to summon the soul repeatedly to inner rejoicing, but also to inner reverence and devotion.' And when the cold mantle of ice has spread over the earth, images of hope will gather in the soul—of how forces of spring and summer will continue, through long ages, to be able to provide a home for the human being, allowing him the chance to develop, out of his own being, those inner faculties and forces which are embedded in his nature. Such is the inward, reverent rejoicing of the soul at the turn of the seasons in spring. It arises from the hope that the earth can endure and enable the human being's capacities and potential to develop to full flower.

These questions can repeatedly surface in the human soul. Will the summer forces be able to overcome winter forces, or at least hold the balance? Will the winter forces perhaps assume such power that they render the earth lifeless before the human soul has completed its earthly mission? Will summer be able to hold the balance against winter? Will the spring always have the strength it needs? These are thoughts that do not come so easily to those whose eyes are focused solely on external nature, but they must, increasingly, come to souls who can see deeply into the spiritual realities of the universe...

What does the moonlight, which shines in the dark like a dream in our sleep, tell us? The esotericist knows that from the active forces of the sun—those sun forces which ever and again renew earth's evolution—as much light and power are taken away as are reflected by the full moon. The human soul may surrender itself to the dreamy magic of moonlit nights, but the esotericist knows that the light which the full moon reflects to earth is subtracted from the light and warmth of the sun.

Thus the full moon is the constant symbol of what is taken from the sun. And when, each spring, sun forces once again penetrate and imbue earthly life, the esotericist knows that with every new spring the sun's forces are weaker than they were the previous spring ... The full moon which appears after the first day of spring, however deeply we may be stirred by its enchantment, is at the same time a stern and solemn reminder of the fact, both earthly and cosmic, that sun forces have dwindled with each new spring, and that we can now never achieve in our earthly missions what we could have done had these forces not been diminished. Realization of this fact places a great question mark in the cosmos ...

[Yet] at the moment Christ died in the body of Jesus of Nazareth[11] on the cross of Golgotha, and united with the earth, a cosmic event occurred within the earthly plane which created a counter-force to the moon's sapping of the sun forces bestowed on the earth from the cosmos. Because the Christ spirit descended to dwell in a human soul, and because his power will spread from that event and imbue the whole course of Earth evolution, compensation has been made for what the moon forces perpetually take from the sun forces that enliven the earth.

... When the waxing forces of the sun, which in their infinite goodness desire always to be giving new life to the earth, stand so close as they do this year[12] to the stern moon spirit which must— through Lucifer[13] and his forces—rob the natural sun of some of its forces; and when the human soul adds Easter Day to the other two days as the moral and spiritual answer to the great cosmic question, then in such years as this the three days stand in wonderful juxtaposition. Good Friday of this year reminds us ... that with every new spring the sun continually loses some of its life-giving power, and that the earth might well have been doomed to die before the human soul had unfolded its full potential. Then the day of the full moon on Easter Saturday harbours a wonderful secret ... Below on the earth the symbol of the newly risen earth force: Christ lying in his grave. We can be deeply moved by the thought of the stern and solemn light of the full moon shining over the Easter grave, as symbol of the penetration of the Christ impulse into the body of the earth. And following this comes Easter Sunday, the sign and symbol of the risen sun, the sun resurrected from the human soul.

Let us feel this trinity in our soul: the outer cosmic sun [equinox] followed by the cosmic moon followed by the moral, spiritual sun. Let us feel this trinity as the symbol of the victory of spirit over matter, of life over death ... Let us realize how the power we call Christ will arise with ever-increasing force in human beings on earth ... so that they learn to sense what must live in them if they are to find their way from the dying earth to higher stages of evolution of the immortal soul that lives on through eternity.

RISING SUN:
NATURE AND RESURRECTION

9. Earth's Rebirth or Spirit's Resurrection?

Extract from a lecture given in Dornach on
12 April 1924

Steiner here revisits the theme of sun and moon, but now accentuates their mutual aid, rather than their opposition, in processes of expansion and contraction in the plant world, mirrored also by flourishing and waning in human life. Describing an ancient autumn festival of resurrection he urges us to sense the earth as a living being, and life itself – both physical and spiritual – as the very essence of Easter, above and beyond death.

The question is, gentlemen: why is the date of Easter set by heavenly standards? It is because, as I have told you, people knew in the past that moon and sun have an influence on everything on earth.

Consider a plant growing in the soil. If this is the soil and you want to have a plant you take a tiny seed and put it in the soil. The whole plant, the whole life of the plant is concentrated in this tiny seed. What becomes of the seed? First of all the root. The plant's

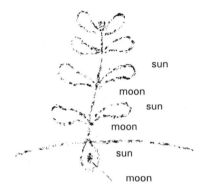

entire life expands into the root. Then it contracts again and grows in contracted form, becoming a stem. It then expands again and leaves develop. The flower follows. And then it contracts again in the seed which will wait for the following year. We thus have expansion, contraction, expansion, contraction, expansion, contraction in the plant.

Every time the plant expands it is the sun which draws forth a leaf, for instance. Every time the plant contracts, being either seed or stem, it is the moon which causes the contraction. The moon is thus active there between the leaves ... We can thus see sun actions alternating with moon actions, powers of sun and powers of moon ... As I have told you, when human beings come into the world, the configuration of their physical bodies depends on the moon; their inner powers, the capacity to change themselves, depend on the sun. I have spoken of this in connection with the Mystery of Golgotha.

You see, this is something people would have known in the past, but it has been forgotten. People would say to themselves: 'When do we have the most powerful activity going on in the spring that enables plants to thrive and grow to be most beneficial for humanity? — When sun and moon work together in the right way.' This is the case when the full moon sends all its rays to the earth for the first time, supporting the sun's rays. This is when sun and moon come together and work together most effectively, the sun having its greatest power in spring, and the moon being at its greatest power every four weeks. Easter thus fell on the Sunday dedicated to the sun, after the first full moon in spring ...

Easter does not have its origin in Christian times but in an ancient pagan festival ... the feast of Adonis. It was celebrated in the artistic, educational and religious centres I have spoken of as the mysteries. Adonis was a kind of image people had of the aspect of the human being that is soul and spirit ... we have to note, however, that the pagans who still took account of the spirit originally celebrated this festival in the autumn.

This autumn feast of Adonis would be celebrated as follows. The image of this eternal, immortal aspect of the human being, of the human soul and spirit, would be immersed in a pond — or in the sea if it was on the coast — and left there for three days. People would sing laments and dirges as the image was lowered into the water. This was a solemn moment, as solemn as the occasions when people had seen a member of their family or a friend die — a real celebration of death. This was always on a day that we would call Friday today. The term used in German, *Karfreitag*, only arose when Christianity reached Central Europe, and is derived from the word *chara*, or lament ...

When the statue was raised again hymns of joy would be sung. For three days emotions of deepest mourning had lived in human souls, and after three days the greatest joy. Those hymns of joy would always be about the god having risen again.

The question is, gentlemen: what was the original meaning of this feast? I must stress again that originally it was celebrated in the autumn ...

The people who created the feast of Adonis said to themselves: 'People should know that a human being does not merely die when his physical body dies but rises again in the world of spirit after three days.' The feast of Adonis was created to remind people of this, year after year. When it was celebrated in the autumn they would say: 'You see, nature is dying. The trees are dropping their leaves and the earth is covered with snow. It grows cold and sharp winds come, the earth loses its fertility. It looks just as a human being does when he dies.' In the case of the earth, however, we must wait until spring for it to rise again, whereas the human being's soul and spirit rises again after three days. This was impressed on people's awareness by a festival of death followed immediately by a festival of resurrection, but in autumn when it could be shown that human beings are the opposite of nature ... when the leaves drop, snow falls and the cold winds blow, people must realize that they are different from nature, for when they die they rise again after three days ... The old Easter festival of Adonis was celebrated when the crops had all been gathered, the grapes had been picked and people were going to rest through the winter. This was the time when they wanted to awaken to the spirit ...

Easter slowly changed to what it is today in the third and fourth centuries AD. Then people no longer understood that there was anything other than nature. They became focused solely on the natural world. And they asked: 'How can we celebrate the resurrection in the autumn? Nothing is resurrected at that time of year!' They no longer knew that the human being rises again in the spirit, and so they said to themselves: 'Nothing rises in autumn, when plants die back; all things rise in

spring, so let us have the Easter festival in spring.'
This is one of the fruits of materialism, though a
materialism in which people still looked up to the
heavens and set the date of Easter according to the
sun and moon ...

At the time Easter was moved to the spring,
people still knew it had to do with a resurrection.
They no longer knew about the resurrection of the
human being but they celebrated the resurrection
that occurred in nature. Gradually this too was
forgotten ...

Easter is intended to be a festival for remember-
ing the resurrection and the immortality of the
human spirit. Seen in this light it will again become
a festival celebrated in our hearts and minds ...
Today people largely relate to the seasons only in
their material aspect, by virtue of the fact that they
put on winter clothes in winter and summer clothes
in summer. People do not know that when spring
comes spiritual powers draw the plants from the
soil, and that spiritual powers also destroy everything in autumn. When this is understood people
will find life everywhere in nature, they will find it
to be full of life. Most people talk nonsense about
the natural world today; for instance they tear a
plant from the ground and botanize, knowing
nothing about its living context. It would be nonsense to tear out a hair and describe it on its own,

for a hair can only grow on an animal or human being ... plants are the hairs of the earth, for the earth is a living organism. And just as human beings need air to live, so the earth needs the spiritual light of the stars. It inhales this in order to live. And just as a person walks around on the earth, so the earth moves around in the cosmos. It dwells in the whole of the universe. The earth is a living entity.

We can say therefore that the least we can achieve when it comes to Easter is to realize that the earth itself is a living entity. It grows young when it lets plants sprout just as a child is young when the baby hair grows. An old man loses his hair just as the earth loses its plants in autumn. That is a life which merely has a different rhythm: youth in spring, old age in autumn, youth again and old age again. It merely takes longer in human beings. And everything in the cosmos really lives like this. The Easter festival can be something for us — at least in the modern world — if we say to ourselves as we see nature coming alive again: 'Death is not the whole reality. Life forms must go through death, but life is the primal element and always conquers death. Easter exists to remind us of life's victory over death, and thus gives us strength.' If people are able to gain strength again in this way they will also be able to use common sense and improve outward social conditions ... But we must first of all have this spiritual quality in the science of the spirit so that we may rediscover harmony with the world of spirit, which is also alive and not dead ...

What we should feel about Easter is this, therefore. Human beings can take up their work again joyfully and with renewed vigour. I'm sure it is often hard for people to look forward to their work, but perhaps this is a place where we can.[14] Here we may have occasion to look forward to our work! I very much wanted to see you again, gentlemen, to tell you this, and to wish you a truly beautiful Easter in the spirit that can be gained from the science of the spirit. I'll see you again after Easter!

10. Beyond Death

Extract from a lecture given in Leipzig on
22 February 1916

*Here Steiner gives us a glimpse into the other side of
death – viewed not as a dead end but as a gateway into
spiritual life. Seen from this perspective death appears as
a triumphant moment, an ascent.*

Whereas, during our physical life, immediate contemplation of our birth can never rise up before our
soul, the moment of death stands before our soul
throughout our life between death and a new birth
if we only look upon it spiritually. We must realize
that we then look upon the moment of death from
the other side. Here on earth death has a terrifying
aspect only because we look upon it as a kind of
dissolution, as an end. But when we look back upon
the moment of death from the other side, from the
spiritual side, then death continually appears to us
as a victory of the spirit, as the spirit that has
extricated itself from the physical. It then appears as
the greatest, most beautiful and significant event.

Moreover, this experience kindles what constitutes our ego consciousness after death. Throughout the time between death and a new birth we have an ego consciousness that not only resembles but far surpasses what we have here during our physical life. We would not have this ego consciousness if we could not look back incessantly, if we would not always see—but from the other side, the spiritual side—that moment in which our spiritual part extricated itself from the physical ...

11. The Resurrection of Letters and Ideas

Extract from a lecture given in Dornach on
22 April 1924

*In these two extracts we can start to see resurrection in a
wider context — as something continually at work in us.
Whether we resurrect meaning from printed letters, or
new ideas from old ones, this is a process of transformation intrinsic to human life. Awareness of this, says
Steiner, can lead us to a sense for the deed of Christ.*

Take any significant work of literature, for example
the *Bhagavadgita* or Goethe's *Faust* or *Iphigenia* — any
work that you admire in fact, and think about its
richness and powerful content. Now how is that
content transmitted to you? Let us assume that it
was transmitted in the usual way, that is, at some
point in your life you read it. Physically speaking,
what precisely did you have before you? Nothing
but combinations of the 26 letters of the alphabet on
paper. The entire, magnificent content comes to you
through mere combinations of these letters. Pro-

vided you can read, something comes to life through these 26 letters that enables you to experience the entire, rich content of Goethe's *Faust*.

Extract from a lecture given in Berlin on
24 April 1917

Since I was 19 I have been continuously occupied with the study of Goethe, but I have never been tempted to write a factual history of his life or even characterize him in the academic sense, for the simple reason that from the very first I felt that what mattered most was that Goethe was still a living force. The physical man Goethe, who was born in 1749 and died in 1832, is less important than the fact that after his death his spirit is still alive amongst us today, not only in the Goethe literature (which is not particularly enlightened) but in the very air we breathe.

This spiritual atmosphere that surrounds us today did not yet exist in people of antiquity. The etheric body, as you know, is separated from the soul after death as a kind of second corpse. But through the Christ impulse, which has informed us ever since the Mystery of Golgotha, the etheric body is now preserved to some extent; it is not wholly dissolved. If we believe ... that Goethe has 'risen' in an etheric body, and if we begin to meditate upon him, then his concepts and ideas become alive in us, and we describe him not as he was but as he is today. The idea of resurrection has then become a living reality and we believe in the resurrection. We can then say that we believe not only in ideas that belong to the past, but also in the living continuity of ideas. This is connected with a profound mystery of modern times. No matter what we may think, so long as we are imprisoned in the physical body our thoughts cannot manifest in the right way. (This does not apply to our feeling and will, but only to our thoughts and concepts.) Great as Goethe was, his ideas were greater than he. That they were unable to rise to greater heights was due to the limitations of his physical body. The moment they are liberated from these limitations of the body and can be developed by someone who has sympathy and understanding for them, they are transformed and acquire new life ... Remember that the form in which ideas first arise in us is not their final form. Believe therefore in the resurrection of ideas! Believe this so firmly that you willingly seek reunion with your forefathers — not those to whom you are linked through blood ties but your spiritual forefathers — and that you may ultimately find them ... Try to fulfil Christ's appeal not to cling to ties of consanguinity, but seek rather a spiritual connection. Then the thought of resurrection can become a living reality in your life and you will believe in resurrection. It is not a question of invoking the name of the Lord incessantly. What matters is that we grasp the living spirit of Christianity, that we hold fast to the vitally important idea of resurrection as a living force. And by drawing support for our inner life from the past in this way, we learn that the past lives on in us, we experience the continuity of the past within us. And then — it is only a question of time — the moment arrives when we are aware of the presence of the Christ. Everything depends on our firm faith in the risen Christ, and the idea of resurrection, so that we can now say: 'We are surrounded by a world of spirit, and the resurrection has become a reality within us.'

12. Physical and Etheric

Extract from a lecture given in Munich on
9 January 1912

*In this passage Steiner speaks of the 'etheric' level of
existence (see note 15) – the force which, imbuing the
physical body with life, can also exist independently of it
for a short while after death. We can get a faint sense of
this subtle, etheric 'body' when we feel uplifted and light.
The phrase 'walking on clouds' gives a feeling of it.*

*After death Christ appeared in etheric form so powerful
and radiant that some were able to see it as a tangible
presence.*

How can we use the principles of spiritual science
to grasp the essence of the Resurrection? What
actually occurred?

Jesus of Nazareth stood by the River Jordan. His
ego separated from the physical, etheric and astral
bodies,[15] and the macrocosmic Christ being descended, took possession of these three bodies and
then lived until 3 April of the year 33, as we can
discover. But this was life of a different kind, for,

from the baptism onwards, this life of Christ in the body of Jesus was a slow dying process. With every advancing stage during these three years one can say that something of the bodily sheaths of Jesus of Nazareth died. Gradually these bodily sheaths died away so that after three years the whole body of Jesus of Nazareth was close to being a corpse, and was only held together by the power of the macrocosmic Christ being. You should not imagine that this body in which Christ lived was, say a year and a half after the Jordan baptism, the same as any other body. An ordinary human soul would immediately have felt this body falling asunder, for it could only be held together by the mighty macrocosmic Christ being. This was a continual, slow death over three years. And this body had reached the verge of dissolution when the Mystery of Golgotha occurred ... Very little was needed for this body to fall to dust in the grave and for the Christ spirit to clothe itself, one can say, in an etheric body that condensed into visibility. Thus the risen Christ was wrapped in an etheric body condensed into visibility. He went about in this way and appeared to those to whom he was able to appear. He was not visible to all since it was really only a condensed etheric body that he bore after resurrection. What had been placed in the grave crumbled into dust. And the most recent occult research confirms that an earthquake did indeed occur. It was striking for me to find a suggestion in the Gospel of St Matthew that an earthquake had occurred after discovering this fact through occult research. The earth opened, the dust of the corpse fell into the opening chasm and united with the whole substance of the earth ... The violent trembling caused by the earthquake shook and scattered the clothes as described — wonderfully — in St John's Gospel.

This is the occult way of grasping the resurrection, which does not need to conflict with what the Gospels say. I have often pointed out that Mary Magdalene did not recognize the Christ when he met her. How could she fail to recognize someone whom she had seen only a few days before, especially when this was such an important individuality as Christ Jesus? When it is related that Mary Magdalene did not recognize him it must be because she encountered him in a different form. She only recognizes him when she hears him speak, as it were. Then she becomes aware of him.[16]

And all details in the Gospels become comprehensible to us from an occult perspective.

Yet someone might object that the risen Christ, when he appeared to his disciples, urged Thomas to touch his wounds. One might therefore think that these wounds were still there and that Christ had

come to the disciples in the same body that had
crumbled into dust. No! Just imagine that someone
has a wound: the etheric body contracts more
tightly at that point, forms a kind of scar. And in
this particularly condensed etheric body, from
which the constituents were drawn with which the
Christ being clothed himself, were especially dense
places — so that Thomas, too, could sense this was a
reality . . .

13. The Etheric Christ

Extract from a lecture given in Basel on
1 October 1911

Pursuing the theme of the etheric level of existence,
Steiner speaks here about the etherealized blood of Christ
uniting with the life body of the earth. By passing through
death and merging with the earth and human destiny,
Christ can reappear in our own time and become visible to
those who develop sensitivity to this level of reality.

Just as in the region of the human heart the blood is
continually being transformed into etheric substance,[17] a similar process takes place in the
macrocosm. We understand this when we turn our
minds to the Mystery of Golgotha — to the moment
when the blood flowed from the wounds of Jesus
Christ.

This blood must not be regarded simply as
chemical substance, but by reason of all that has
been said about the nature of Jesus of Nazareth it
must be recognized as something altogether
unique. When it flowed from his wounds a sub-

stance was imparted to the earth which in uniting
with it constituted an event of the greatest possible
significance for all future ages of the earth's evolution—and it could take place only once. What
came of this blood in the ages that followed? The
very same as occurs in the human heart. In the
course of human evolution this blood passes
through a process of 'etherization'. And just as our
human blood streams upwards from the heart as
ether, so since the Mystery of Golgotha the etherized blood of Christ Jesus has been present in the
earth's ether. The etheric body of the earth is permeated by the blood—now transformed—which
flowed on Golgotha. This is supremely important. If
what thus came to pass through Christ Jesus had
not taken place, the human being's condition on the
earth could only have been as previously described.[18] But since the Mystery of Golgotha it has
always been possible for the etheric blood of Christ
to flow together with the streams flowing in us from
below upwards, from heart to head.

Because the etherized blood of Jesus of Nazareth
is present in the etheric body of the earth, it
accompanies the etherized human blood streaming
upwards from the heart to the brain, so that ... the
human bloodstream unites with the bloodstream of
Christ Jesus. A union of these two streams can,
however, come about only if a person is able to

unfold true understanding of what is contained in the Christ impulse.[19] Otherwise there can be no union and the two streams then mutually repel each other, thrust each other away. In every epoch of Earth evolution, understanding must be acquired *in the form suitable for that epoch* ... In our age what matters is that people should recognize the need for the knowledge contained in the science of the spirit, and be able to fire the streams flowing from heart to brain in such a way that this knowledge can be understood.

If this occurs, individuals will be able to receive and comprehend the event that has its beginning in the twentieth century: the appearance of the etheric being of Christ as opposed to the physical Christ of Palestine. For we have now reached the point of time when the etheric Christ enters into the life of the earth and will become visible — at first to a small number of individuals through a form of natural clairvoyance. Then in the course of the next three thousand years he will become visible to ever greater numbers of people ... But this will depend upon them learning to be alert to the moment when Christ draws near to them. In only a few decades from now it will happen, particularly to those who are young — there are many signs of this already — that some individual here or there has certain experiences. If he has sharpened his vision through studying spiritual science he may become aware that suddenly someone has come near to help him, to make him alert to this or that ... Many a person will have this experience when sitting silent in his room, heavy-hearted and oppressed, not knowing which way to turn. The door will open and the etheric Christ will appear and speak words of consolation to him. The Christ will become a living comforter to human beings ...

Thus we realize what a tremendous occurrence it was for Christ to live three years on the earth in a specially prepared human body, so that he might be visible to physical eyes. Through what occurred during those three years people have grown ready to behold the Christ who will move among them in an etheric body, who will participate in earthly life as truly and effectively as did the physical Christ in Palestine.

14. Harmony from Chaos

A lecture given in Berlin on 12 April 1906

The last lecture in this section, reproduced in its entirety, recapitulates many of the themes touched on so far, then proceeds to a description of the unfathomable wisdom built into our bodies, of which we are largely unaware. Evolution is seen as a gradual process of increasing awareness, in which the cosmic wisdom that fashioned us dawns in the conscious soul. Easter, says Steiner, embodies the moment of awakening – of spiritual resurrection from matter – when harmony arises from chaos.

In many different ways, Goethe often described a feeling of which he was persistently aware. He said, in effect: When I see the irrelevance manifesting in the passions, emotions and actions of human beings I feel the strong urge to turn to all-powerful nature and be comforted by her majesty and consistency. In such utterances Goethe was referring to what humanity has brought to expression in the festivals since time immemorial. The festivals are reminders of a striving to turn away from the chaotic life of human passions, urges and activities to the consistent, harmonious processes and events of nature. Easter is one such festival. For Christians today, Easter is the festival of the resurrection of their saviour. It was celebrated not only as a symbol of nature's awakening but also of the human being's awakening. The human being was urged to awaken to the reality underlying certain inner experiences.

In ancient Egypt we find a festival connected with Osiris. In Greece a spring festival was celebrated in honour of Dionysus. There were similar celebrations in Asia Minor where the resurrection or return of a God was associated with the reawakening of nature. In India, too, there are festivals dedicated to the god Vishnu. Brahmanism speaks of three aspects of the deity, namely, Brahma, Vishnu and Shiva. The supreme God Brahma is referred to as the great Architect of the world, who brings about order and harmony. Vishnu is described as a kind of redeemer or liberator, awakening slumbering life. And Shiva, originally, was the being who blesses the slumbering life that has been awakened by Vishnu and raises it to whatever heights can be reached. A particular festival was therefore dedicated to Vishnu. It was said that he goes to sleep at the time of year when we celebrate Christmas and wakes at the time of our Easter festival. Those who adhere to this eastern teaching celebrate the days of their festival in a characteristic way. For the whole of this period they abstain from certain foods and drinks, for example all pod-producing plants, all kinds of oils, all salt, intoxicating beverages and meat. This is the way in which people prepare themselves to understand what was actually celebrated in the Vishnu festival, the resurrection of the god and the awakening of all nature.

The Christmas festival, too, the old festival of the winter solstice, is connected with particular occurrences in nature. The days leading up to this point of time become progressively shorter and the sun's power steadily weakens. But from Christmas onwards greater and greater warmth streams from the sun. Christmas is the festival of the reborn sun.

Christianity wished to establish a link with these ancient festivals. The date of the birth of Jesus can be seen as the day when the sun's power again begins to increase in the heavens. In the Easter festival the spiritual significance of the world's saviour was thus connected with the physical sun and with the awakening and returning life in spring.

As in the case of all ancient festivals the fixing of the date of the Easter festival was also determined by a certain constellation in the heavens. In the first century AD the symbol of Christianity was the

Cross, with a lamb at its foot. Lamb and Ram (Aries) are synonymous. During the epoch when preparation was being made for Christianity, the sun was rising in the constellation of the Ram or Lamb. As we know, the sun moves through all the zodiacal constellations, each year progressing a little further than the year before (precession of the equinoxes). Approximately seven hundred years before the coming of Christ the sun began to rise in the constellation of the Ram. Before then it rose in the constellation of the Bull (Taurus). In those times people expressed what seemed to them important about the evolution of humanity in the symbol of the bull, because the sun then rose in that constellation. When the rising sun moved forward into the constellation of the Ram or Lamb, the ram became a figure of significance in saga and myth. Jason brings the golden fleece from Colchis. Christ Jesus himself is called the Lamb of God, and in the earliest period of Christianity he is portrayed as the Lamb at the foot of the Cross. Thus the Easter festival is obviously connected with the constellation of the Lamb or Ram. The festival of the resurrection of the Redeemer is celebrated at the time when, in nature, everything awakens to new life after lying as though dead through the winter months.

Between the Christmas and Easter festivals there is certainly a correspondence, but in their relation to the events of nature there is a great difference. In its deepest significance Easter is always felt to be the festival of the greatest mystery connected with the human being. It is not merely a festival celebrating the reawakening of nature but is essentially more than that. It is an expression of the significance in Christianity of the resurrection after death. Vishnu's sleep sets in at the time when, in winter, the sun begins to ascend once more. It is precisely then that we celebrate our Christmas festival. When the Easter festival is celebrated the sun is continuing its ascent, which started from the Christmas festival onwards.

We must penetrate very deeply into the mysteries of human nature if we are to understand the feelings of initiates when they wished to give expression to the true facts underlying the Easter festival. The human being is in a sense twofold: on the one hand he is a being of soul and spirit, and on the other a physical being. The physical being is actually a confluence of all the phenomena of nature surrounding us. Paracelsus speaks of the human being as the quintessence of all that is outspread in external nature. Nature contains the letters as it were, and the human being forms the word composed of those letters.

When we observe a human being closely we recognize the wisdom that is displayed in his constitution and structure. Not without reason has the body been called the temple of the soul. All the laws that can be observed in the dead stone, in the living plant, are assembled into a unity in the human being. When we study the marvellous structure of the human brain with its countless cells cooperating among themselves in a way that enables all the thoughts and sentient experiences filling the human soul to come to expression, we realize with what supreme wisdom the human body has been constructed. But in the surrounding world too we behold an array of crystallized wisdom. When we look out into the world, applying what knowledge we possess to the laws in operation there, and then turn to observe the human being, we see all nature concentrated in him. That is why sages have spoken of the human being as a microcosm of the great macrocosm spread out in nature.

It was in this sense that we can understand Schiller's words to Goethe in a letter of 23 August 1794:

You take the whole of nature into your purview in order to shed light upon a single sentence; in the totality of her (nature's) manifold external manifestations you seek the explanation of the individual. From the simple organism you proceed step by step to the more complex, in order finally to build up by a natural process from the materials of nature's whole edifice the most complex organism of all—the human being.

The wonderful organization of the body enables the human soul to have sight of the surrounding world. Through the senses the soul beholds the world and endeavours to fathom the wisdom by which that world has been constructed.

With this in mind let us now think of a fairly undeveloped human being. The wisdom manifesting in his bodily structure is the greatest that can possibly be imagined. The sum total of divine wisdom is concentrated in a single human body. Yet in this body there dwells a childlike soul, scarcely able to understand the mysterious forces operating in his own heart, brain and blood. The soul develops slowly to a higher stage where it can understand the powers that have been at work with the object of producing the human body. This body itself bears the hallmark of an infinitely long past. The physical human being is the crown of the rest of Creation. What was it that inevitably had to precede the building of the human body? What had to occur before cosmic wisdom could become concentrated in this human being? Cosmic wisdom is concentrated in the body of a human being standing before us, yet it is in the *soul* of an undeveloped human being that this wisdom first starts to come to expression. The soul barely dreams of the great cosmic thoughts according to which the human being has evolved. Nevertheless we can glimpse a future when people will be conscious of the reality of soul and spirit still at present lying within us as though asleep. Cosmic thought has been active throughout ages without number, has been continually active in nature with the purpose of finally producing the crown of all its creative work—the human body.

Cosmic wisdom is now slumbering in the human body in order subsequently to acquire self-knowledge in the human soul, in order to build an eye in the human being through which to be recognized—cosmic wisdom without, cosmic wisdom within, creative in the present as it was in the past and will be in future time. Gazing forwards we glimpse the ultimate goal, surmising the future existence of a great soul which understands and finally embodies and liberates the cosmic wisdom that existed from the very beginning. Our deepest feelings rise up within us full of expectation when we contemplate the past and future in this way.

When the soul begins to recognize the wonders accomplished by cosmic wisdom, and when clarity and illumination have been achieved, the sun may well be accepted as the worthiest symbol of this inner awakening. Through the gate of the senses the soul is able to gaze into the external world because the sun illumines the contents of that world. Fundamentally speaking, what we perceive in the external world is the result of the sun's reflected light. It is the sun that wakens in the soul the power to behold the external world. An awakening soul, one that is beginning to recognize the seasons as expressions of cosmic thought, sees the rising sun as its liberation.

When the sun again begins its ascent, when the days lengthen, the soul turns to the sun, declaring: 'To you I owe the possibility of discerning, outspread around me, the cosmic thought that sleeps within me and within all other human beings.'

Such an individual is now able to survey his former existence, before he came to grasp the activities of cosmic thought in the world. We are more ancient than our senses. Through spiritual investigation we can eventually reach back to the point in the far past when the human senses were first coming into existence, when they were only present in the most rudimentary form. At that stage the senses were not yet doors enabling the soul to become aware of its environment.

Schopenhauer realized this, and in stating that the visible world first came into existence when an eye was there to behold it he was referring to the turning point when the human being acquired the faculty of sensory perception.

The sun formed the eye for itself and for the light. In still earlier times when the human being did not yet have external vision he nevertheless had inner vision. In the primeval ages of evolution outer objects did not give rise to ideas or mental concepts in the human being but rose up in him from within. Vision in those ancient times was vision in the astral light.[20] Human beings were then endowed with a faculty of dim, shadowy clairvoyance, and it was by means of this dim and hazy faculty that they beheld the world of the gods and formed their conceptions of the gods accordingly. This dim clairvoyance faded into darkness and gradually disappeared altogether. It was extinguished by the strong light of the physical sun which made the physical world visible to the senses. Astral vision then died away altogether.

When we gaze into the future we realize that astral vision must return, but at a higher stage. What has now been extinguished for the sake of physical vision will return and combine with physical vision in order to generate clairvoyance — clear seeing in the fullest sense. In the future a still more lucid consciousness will accompany our waking vision. To physical vision will be added vision in the astral light, that is to say, perception with soul organs. Those whom we regard as humanity's foremost individuals are those who, through lives of renunciation, have developed in themselves a condition which later becomes established in all. Such exemplars of humanity already possess the astral vision that renders soul and spirit visible to them.

The Easter festival is connected spiritually not only with the awakening of the sun but with the unfolding of the plant world in spring. Just as the grain of corn falls into the soil and slumbers, eventually awakening anew, so the astral light in the human constitution was obliged to slumber in order to be reawoken in the fullness of time. The symbol of the Easter festival is the grain of corn, the seed which sacrifices itself to enable a new plant to come into existence. In the life of nature this is the sacrifice of one phase so that a new one may begin. Sacrifice and evolving are interwoven in the Easter festival.

Richard Wagner was conscious of the beauty and majesty of this thought. In the year 1857, at Villa Wesendonck by Lake Zurich, while he was looking at the spectacle of awakening nature, the thought came to him of the Saviour who had died and awoken, the thought of Jesus Christ, and also of Parsifal who was seeking for what is most holy in the human soul.

All the exemplars of humanity who know how the higher life of the human being awakens out of our lower nature have understood the Easter thought. Dante, too, in his *Divine Comedy*, describes his awakening on a Good Friday. This is brought to our attention at the very beginning of the poem. It was in his 36th year, that is to say, the middle of his life,[21] that Dante had the great vision he describes. Seventy years are thought to be the normal span of life, and 35 therefore marks the midpoint. The first 35 years of life are reckoned to be the period devoted to the development of physical experience. At the age of 35 the human being has reached the degree of maturity when spiritual experience can be added to physical experience. He is ready for perception of the spiritual world.

When all the waking, nascent forces of physical life have been consolidated, the time begins for spiritual awakening. Thus Dante connects his vision with the Easter festival.

Whereas the original point at which the sun's power starts to increase is celebrated in the Christmas festival, the Easter festival takes place at the midpoint of the sun's increasing trajectory. This was also the point when, in the middle of his life, Dante became aware of the dawn of spiritual life within himself. The Easter festival is rightly celebrated at the middle point of the sun's ascent, for this corresponds to the time when the slumbering astral light will reawaken in the human being. The seed of corn is an image of what arises in the human being when what occultists call the astral light is born within him. Therefore Easter is also the festival of the resurrection that takes place in our inner nature.

It has been thought that there is a kind of contradiction between what a Christian sees in the Easter festival and the idea of karma.[22] There seems at first to be a contradiction between the idea of karma and redemption by the Son of Man.[23] Those who have little grasp of the fundamentals of anthroposophical[24] thought may see a contradiction between the redemption wrought by Christ Jesus and the idea of karma. Such people say that the thought of redemption by the God contradicts the truth of self-redemption through karma. But the truth is that they understand neither the Easter thought of redemption nor the thought of the justice of karma. It would certainly not be right if someone seeing another person suffer were to say to him, 'You yourself were the cause of this suffering,' and were to refuse to help him because karma must take its course. This would be a misunderstanding of karma. What the law of karma says is this: help the person who is suffering, for you are actually there to do so. You do not violate karmic necessity by helping your fellow human beings. On the contrary, you are helping him to bear his karma. You are then yourself a redeemer of suffering.

Likewise, instead of a single individual, a whole group of people can be helped, and by helping them we become part of their karma.

When a being as all-powerful as Christ Jesus comes to the help of the human race, his sacrificial death becomes a factor in the collective karma of mankind. He could bear and give aid to this karma, and we may be sure that the redemption through him plays an essential role in its fulfilment.

The thought of resurrection and redemption can in reality be fully grasped only through a knowledge of spiritual science. In the Christianity of the future there will be no contradiction between the idea of karma and redemption. Because cause and effect belong together in the life of the spirit, this great deed of sacrifice by Christ Jesus must also have an effect in the life of mankind.

Spiritual science adds depth to the thought underlying the Easter festival—a thought that is inscribed and can be read in the world of the stars.

In the middle of his span of life the human being is surrounded by inharmonious, bewildering conditions. But he knows too that just as the world came forth from chaos so will harmony eventually proceed from his still disorderly inner nature. The inner saviour in the human being, the bringer of unity and harmony to counter all disharmony, will arise and act with the ordered regularity of the course of the planets around the sun. May everyone be reminded by the Easter festival of the resurrection of the spirit within the human being's present nature.

GOLGOTHA: THE CENTRAL DEED OF EVOLUTION

15. Descending to Ascend

Extract from a lecture given in Dornach on
1 April 1923

*The descent of Christ into 'hell' is an image of his pro-
found engagement with the very depths of our earthly
nature, including the evil slumbering there. Through this
descent – as it were illuminating the darknesses of the
soul – Christ also opens the way to spiritual ascent.*

Human beings saw the Christ arise in their realm.
The gods saw the Christ forsake the heavenly world
and plunge down amongst humanity. For human
beings the Christ appeared; for certain spiritual
beings he vanished. Only when he passed through
the Resurrection did he appear again to certain
supersensible spiritual beings, now shining out to
them from the earth like a star, radiating from earth
into the world of spirit. Spiritual beings mark the
Mystery of Golgotha by saying: 'A star began to
shine out from the earth into the realm of spirit.'
And it was felt to be of immense importance for the
spiritual world that Christ had submerged into a

human body and passed through death in this body. For by doing so he was able, immediately after death, to undertake something which his former divine companions could not possible have accomplished.

These former divine companions confronted, as an inimical world, what in earlier times was called 'hell'. The working and efficacy of these spiritual beings stopped short at the gates of this region. These spiritual beings work upon us but our own forces extend down into hell. What this means is simply that, subconsciously, we descend into the ahrimanic[25] realm of forces in winter, and these ahrimanic forces ascend in us in spring. The divine spiritual beings felt this to be a world alien and opposed to them. They saw it rise out of the earth and felt it to be very much a problem. But they themselves had only an indirect connection to it through the human being, and could only observe it at one remove as it were. But because Christ descended to the earth, and assumed human form, he was able to descend into the realm of these ahrimanic forces and overcome them. This is expressed in the Creed as the 'descent into hell'.

This descent into hell provides the opposite pole to the Resurrection. This is what Christ has done for humanity: by descending from divine heights and taking on human form, he became able to descend into the realm to whose danger we are exposed, into which other gods, who had not passed through human death, could not descend. In his way the Christ gained victory over death, and thus, as the opposite pole to the descent into hell, opened the ascent into the world of spirit despite remaining on earth. Christ united himself with humanity to the extent of descending right into the ahrimanic realm to which we are exposed as human beings ... Thus in the Easter thought we see united in a certain way the descent into the region known as hell and through this descent the winning of the heavenly regions for humanity's further evolution.

All this belongs to a true conception of Easter. But what would this conception be if it cannot become living in us?

16. From Christmas to Easter

Extract from a lecture given in Dornach on
27 March 1921

*Here Steiner returns to a prevailing theme of his, the loss
of humanity's spiritual vision as it engaged increasingly
with physical reality in the course of evolution. While this
descent (and decline) was necessary, the journey of ascent
made possible by Christ is now essential.*

There is a significant contrast between the Christmas thought and the Easter thought. Understanding the contrast and also the living
relationship between them will lead to an experience which, in a certain way, embraces the whole
riddle of human existence.

The Christmas thought points to birth. Through
birth our eternal being enters the world from which
the material, physical constitution is derived. The
Christmas thought therefore links us with the
supersensible. Together with all its other associa-
tions it points us to the one pole of our existence
where as physical, material beings we connect back

to the spiritual and supersensible. The birth of a human being can never, therefore, be explained wholly by a science based solely upon observation of material existence.

The thought underlying the Easter festival lies at the other pole of human experience. In the course of western civilization's development, this Easter thought increasingly assumed a form which paved the way for western materialistic thinking. The Easter thought can be grasped, in a more abstract way to begin with, when we realize that the immortal, spiritual, supersensible essence of the human being, which cannot be born in the real sense, descends from spiritual worlds and is clothed in the human physical body, and that from the very beginning of physical existence the working of the spirit within the physical body actually leads this physical body towards death. The thought of death is therefore implicit in that of birth.

On other occasions I have said that we must see what is at work in the human head and nervous system as nothing other than a continual death process, counteracted only by the life forces in the rest of the organism. The moment the forces of death—which are continually present in the head and enable us to think—get the upper hand over our transient, mortal nature, then actual death occurs.

The thought of death is therefore really only the other side of the coin of birth, and cannot be an essential part of the Easter thought. At the time when the early, Pauline forms of Christianity still drew upon eastern wisdom, it was not to the death but the resurrection of Christ Jesus that people's minds were drawn, for instance by those powerful words of Paul: 'If Christ be not risen then is your faith dead.'

The Resurrection, the triumphant victory over death, the overcoming of death, was the essence of the Easter thought in the early form of Christianity still influenced by eastern wisdom. On the other hand there are pictures in which Christ Jesus is portrayed as the Good Shepherd, watching over the eternal concerns of the human being as he sleeps through mortal existence. In early Christianity we are continually directed to the words of the Gospel: 'He whom ye seek is not here.' Expanding this we might say: 'Seek him in spiritual worlds, not in the physical, material world. For if you seek him in the world of physical matter you will simply find that he whom you seek is no longer here.'

The all-embracing wisdom which in the first centuries of Christendom still endeavoured to grasp and penetrate the Mystery of Golgotha and all that it involved was gradually submerged by the materialism of the West ... The original eastern concept of religion came to be bound up with the concept of the state that was developing in the West. In the fourth century AD Christianity became a state religion—in other words, there crept into Christianity something that is not religion at all.

Julian the Apostate, who was no Christian but nevertheless a deeply religious man, could not accept what Christianity had become under Constantine. And so we see how, in the fusion of Christianity with Rome's declining culture, western materialism begins to make its appearance—very slightly at first but nevertheless perceptibly. And under this influence there appeared a picture of Christ Jesus that at the beginning simply was not there, was not part of Christianity in its original form: the picture of Christ Jesus as the crucified one, the man of sorrows, brought to his death by the indescribable suffering that was his lot.

This made a breach in the whole outlook of the Christian world. For the picture which from then on persisted through the centuries—the picture of Christ agonizing on the cross—is the Christ who could no longer be comprehended in his spiritual nature but his bodily nature only. And the greater the emphasis that was laid on the signs of suffering in the human body, the more perfect was the skill with which art succeeded at different periods in portraying these sufferings, the more firmly were

the seeds of materialism planted in Christian feeling. The crucifix is the expression of this transition
to Christian materialism. This in no way gainsays
the profundity and significance with which art
portrayed the sufferings of the Redeemer. Nevertheless it is a fact that through this picture of the
Redeemer suffering and dying on the cross human
beings gradually lost sight of a truly spiritual conception of Christianity ...

An attitude of mind arose that could banish the
image of the victorious spirit of the Redeemer rising
triumphant over death, and leave only that of the
grave. This was the same attitude of mind which, in
the year 869, at the Eighth Ecumenical Council in
Constantinople, declared belief in the spirit to be
heretical, decreeing that man has only a body and
soul, the soul merely having certain spiritual
qualities ...

The Good Friday festival and the Easter festival
of resurrection were largely combined. Even in
times when human beings were not yet so arid, so
devoid of understanding, Good Friday became a
festival in which the Easter thought was transformed in an altogether egotistic way. Wallowing
in pain, steeping the soul voluptuously in pain
was, for centuries, associated with the Good Friday thought—which should really only have
formed the background to the Easter thought. But

people became less and less able to grasp the Easter thought in its true form. The same humanity which had accepted the principle that the human being consists only of body and soul, needed to sustain its emotional life through the picture of the dying Redeemer. This image was the reflection of humanity's own physical suffering, and served as a contrasting background against which people could experience, at least outwardly, what they had once experienced directly: that the living spirit must always be victorious over everything that can befall the physical body. People needed, first, the picture of the martyr's death, in order to experience, by way of contrast, the true Easter thought.

The way in which vision and experience of the spirit gradually faded from western culture must profoundly touch our feelings. We can certainly admire, though with a certain feeling of tragedy, all the artistic portrayals of the man of sorrows on the cross. Haphazard thoughts and casual feelings about what is needed in our time are not sufficient. We must perceive with the greatest clarity the decline that has taken place in western culture in respect of understanding of the spirit. We need to recognize today that even the greatest achievements in a certain domain are something that humanity must now surmount. The whole of our western culture needs the Easter thought, needs in other words to be lifted to the spirit ...

We live in an age in which we must experience the resurrection of our own being in the spirit. We must therefore learn to understand the importance of the Easter thought for us, in all its depths ... We need the Christ as a supersensible, super-earthly being who nevertheless entered the stream of earthly evolution. This thought is the sun to all our human thinking, and we must fight our way through to it ... Easter must become an inner festival in which we celebrate in ourselves the victory of the spirit over the body. As history should not be disregarded we shall not ignore the figure of the pain-racked Jesus, the man of sorrows on the cross; but above the cross we must behold the victor who remains unaffected by either birth or death, and who alone can lead our vision up to the eternal pastures of life in the spirit. Only so shall we draw near again to the true being of Christ ...

We need the Christ for whom we can seek in our inmost being, because when we truly seek him he at once appears. We need the Christ who enters our will, warming, kindling, strengthening it for deeds demanded of us for the sake of human evolution. We need not the suffering Christ but the Christ who hovers above the cross looking down upon what has ended there, which is no longer a living reality ...

The Good Friday mood, as well as the Easter mood, needs to be transformed. The Good Friday mood must be one that finds in contemplation of the dying Jesus only the other aspect of birth. We lose sight of the full reality if we do not recognize death as implicit in birth. If we can feel that the mood of death associated with Good Friday is merely the other aspect of the entrance of the child into the world at birth, we can make the right preparation for the mood of Easter, which consists solely in the knowledge that whatever the mortal frame I have been born into, my real being is both unborn and deathless. In our own eternal being we must unite with the Christ who came into the world and cannot die, who, when he beholds the man of sorrows on the cross, is looking down upon something other than himself . . .

We have to seek the one who *is* here, by turning at Easter time to the spirit which can be given to us only in the image of the Resurrection. Then we shall be able to properly pass from the Good Friday mood of suffering to the spiritual mood of Easter Day. In this Easter mood we shall also be able to find the strength with which our will must be imbued if the forces of decline are to be countered by those which lead humanity upwards. We need the forces that can bring about this ascent. And the moment we truly understand the Easter thought of resurrection it will bring us warmth and illumination, and kindle within us the forces needed for the future evolution of mankind.

17. The Reality of Christ's Deed

Extract from a lecture given in Berlin on
1 January 1909

*Here Steiner paints a dire image of what the fate of the
earth and humanity would have been without Christ.
Against this bleak perspective we can gain a clearer view
of the significance of Christ's deed for humanity.*

Although Christ appeared only later, he was always
present in the spiritual sphere of the earth. Already
in the ancient oracles of Atlantis, the priests of those
oracles spoke of the 'spirit of the sun', of Christ ...
In the spiritual world he was always to be found,
working in and from the spiritual world ... then he
came himself to the earth, and we know what this
has meant for humanity ... we have spoken of the
significance of the event of Golgotha and of its effect
also upon those who at that time were in the
spiritual world, not incarnate in earthly bodies. We
know that at the moment on Golgotha when the
blood flowed from the wounds, the Christ spirit
appeared in the underworld, flooding the whole

world of spirit with radiance and light; we have said that the appearance of Christ on the earth is the event of supreme importance, also for the world through which human beings pass between death and a new birth.

The impulse radiating from Christ is in the fullest sense *reality*. We need only ask ourselves what would have become of the earth had Christ not appeared. Precisely from the opposite picture — an earth without Christ — you can grasp the significance of Christ's coming. Let us suppose that Christ had not come, that the Mystery of Golgotha had not taken place.

Before Christ's coming, the condition in the spiritual world of human souls who were the most advanced, who had acquired the deepest interest in earthly life, was truly expressed by the saying of the Greeks: 'Better a beggar in the upper world than a king in the realm of the Shades.' For before the event of Golgotha souls in the spiritual world after death felt completely isolated, enveloped in darkness. The spiritual world in all its gleaming clarity was not transparent to those who entered it through the portal of death. Each one felt isolated, thrust back into himself as though a wall were between himself and every other soul. And this feeling of isolation would have become more and more intense. The human being would have hardened within the ego, would have been thrown back upon himself, nor could he have found any bridge to the others. And egotism, already intense, would have increased beyond all telling with every new incarnation.

Earth existence would increasingly have turned human beings into utter egotists. There would have been no prospect of brotherhood on the earth or of inner harmony among souls; for with every journey through the spiritual world, stronger influence would have penetrated the ego. That is what would have happened to an earth without Christ. That the way from soul to soul will be found again, that it has been made possible for the mighty force of brotherhood to pour over all humanity — this is due to Christ's coming, to the event of Golgotha. Therefore Christ is the power that has enabled human beings to turn earth existence, ultimately, to good account, in other words to give karma[26] its true configuration — for karma must be worked out on the *earth*. That we can find in ourselves the capacity to progress through our karma in physical existence, that advancing evolution is possible for us — all this we owe to the Christ event, to the presence of Christ in the earthly realm.

And so we see many diverse forces and beings working together in the evolution of humanity. Had Christ not come to earth the human being would have been engulfed in error, because, having hardened within himself, he would have become as it were a self-contained world, knowing nothing of other beings, entirely self-enclosed, driven into that condition by error and sin.

Christ is truly the light which leads us out of error and sin, the light which enables us to find the way upwards again ...

18. The Heaviest Guilt and the Greatest Good Fortune

Extract from a lecture given in Berlin on
3 April 1917

Steiner here emphasizes the importance of a threefold view of the human being – body, soul and spirit, rather than the unmediated duality of body and spirit alone – for understanding the Golgotha event. This echoes his view of Christ as a mediating presence of equilibrium between two potentially negative poles – submersion in matter (Ahriman) and flight from the earth (Lucifer). The human soul, centred in the thinking heart, is poised between these two necessary but dangerous extremes, and Christ provides the necessary balance without denying either of them.

Like medieval mystics such as Meister Eckhart, Steiner also presents us with a powerful paradox at the core of the Easter event: humanity's guilt in this event coincides with the good fortune which arose from it. Elsewhere Steiner has pointed out that a terrible wrong on one level can give rise to a self-correcting impetus for good. Here he suggests that the power of forgiveness is the key – a love which, rather than condemning, allows ignorance and immorality to be transformed.

The Mystery of Golgotha ... will be the subject of our enquiry today.

Let us recall the main points for consideration. On the last occasion I mentioned that in order to arrive at a true understanding of the world we must study the threefold division of the cosmos and the human being in the light of the three principles of body, soul and spirit ...

There is no doubt that this idea of the human being's threefold nature has been suppressed. The spirit, it is true, has often been a focus of discussion today, but such discussions are little more than empty words. People are largely unable today to distinguish between mere words and realities ...

We cannot understand the essential nature of the Mystery of Golgotha if we decide to reject the threefold nature of the human being, of body, soul and spirit ...

A few centuries before the Mystery of Golgotha the human being had entered on a stage of evolution when something akin to a mist shrouded the soul whenever the spirit was mentioned. This mist was not so dense then as it is now, but the first signs of the corruption of human thinking in relation to things of the spirit were already apparent at that time ... Over the centuries the human soul had changed and was no longer the same as it had been in primeval times ... In the period shortly before the

Mystery of Golgotha people ... looked back to ancient times and said to themselves: ... 'In the course of hundreds and thousands of years the condition of the soul has grown progressively worse and the body has suffered continuous corruption. Thus it is increasingly difficult for us to find our way back to the spirit. The further evolution advances, the more the body is corrupted by the soul, and the more the seeds of death are sown in the body. And a time will come when it will no longer be possible for human beings, once they have lived their allotted span, to find their way back to the spiritual world.'

In ancient times it was this moment that was anticipated with fear and dread. People felt that after countless generations a generation would arise whose souls would so corrupt the body and sow the poisonous seeds of death that the human being would be divorced from his spiritual heritage ...

When we touch upon these questions we become aware of the unplumbed depth of feelings and emotions which were once characteristic of a particular epoch in human evolution. Today people generally do not have the slightest inkling of the inner conflicts with which these people of earlier times wrestled. Though they may have been totally illiterate and have known nothing of what we call

culture today, yet they could not escape these feelings. And in the mystery schools, which preserved
the old traditions derived from ancient clairvoyant
insight, the neophytes were told that if evolution
were to continue unchanged, if the effects of original sin were to be prolonged, a time would come
when human souls turned from God to immersion
in a world of materialism of their own creation, and
would progressively corrupt the physical body and
rapidly hasten the process of death ...

From the 'Fall' until the Mystery of Golgotha, the
human being experienced a progressive decline of
his spiritual forces. The forces of corruption had
increasingly invaded his soul and threatened to
make him into a soulless automaton. But from the
Mystery of Golgotha until the end of the cycle of
Earth evolution all that was lost before will gradually be retrieved again ...

Before this could be realized it was necessary to
overcome the power which had caused the moral
corruption of the soul; and this power was overcome by the decisive event of Golgotha. How did
the early Christians who still possessed occult
knowledge understand the last words of Christ on
the cross? They were living in hope and expectation
of an external event that would bring to an end this
corrupting influence of the soul. The cry of Christ
on the cross 'It is finished' was a sign to them that

the time had now come when the corrupting power of the soul was a thing of the past. It was a miraculous event fraught with vast and unsuspected mysteries, for tremendous questions are involved when we think about the Mystery of Golgotha. When we pursue our studies further we shall find that it is impossible to think of the Mystery of Golgotha without also thinking of the risen Christ. The risen Christ—that is essential. And in one of his most profound utterances St Paul says: 'If Christ be not risen then all our faith is in vain.' The risen Christ is unique to Christianity and inseparable from it. The death of Christ is also an integral part of Christianity. But how is this death portrayed? And how must it be portrayed? An innocent man was put to death, suffered and died. Those who crucified him clearly bear a heavy burden of guilt, for he who died was innocent. What was the significance of this guilt for mankind? It brought them salvation. For had Christ not died upon the cross, mankind could not have been saved. In the Crucifixion we are faced with a unique event. The death of Christ on the cross was the greatest boon bestowed upon mankind.[27] And the heaviest guilt that mankind has taken upon itself is this, that Christ was crucified. Thus the heaviest guilt coincides with the greatest good fortune.

Superficial minds will no doubt pay little attention to this. But for those who probe deeper this question is fraught with profound mystery. The most heinous crime in the history of the world proved to be the salvation of humanity. Now we must understand this enigma, or at least try to understand it, if we are to comprehend the Mystery of Golgotha. And the key to the solution of this enigma is found in the exemplary words spoken by Christ on the cross: 'Forgive them, Father, for they know not what they do.' The right understanding of these words provides the answer to the cardinal question: why did the most heinous crime become the source of humanity's salvation?

If you reflect upon this you will realize that one must take the threefold nature of the human being into account in order to understand the Mystery of Golgotha, for Christ died in order to redeem human souls. He reclaims the human souls that would have been lost but for his advent. Morality would have vanished from the earth, and the spirit inhabiting a soulless, automaton body would have become the victim of amoral compulsion and necessity. Humanity would have been divorced from the soul's mediating and feeling experience ... The significance of Christ for human souls is that he demonstrates once again that the human being is a threefold being of body, soul and spirit, and that an inner relationship exists between objective events and moral events. And we shall never fully understand this relationship unless we accept the idea of the threefold nature of the human being ...

19. Freeing the Soul from the Destiny of the Body

Extract from a lecture given in The Hague on
13 April 1912

In this extract Steiner juxtaposes an event (Golgotha) that broke all earthly laws with insight into the transformation in us necessary to perceive it. Continuing his 'threefold' view of the human being, Steiner makes this more specific here by describing how the soul inhabits different spheres of the body in different ways and, paradoxically, is most free in the most material region, the metabolic system. He relates this to the Holy Communion ritual, whose original aim was to enable human beings to unite with Christ in their deepest will forces. While this insight has largely been lost, it remains a reality that Christ is a liberating force who saves the soul from the body's destined death, and can thus help engender the very mode of understanding we need to perceive his presence.

The importance of the Mystery of Golgotha can only be truly appreciated when we envisage two streams of evolution in earthly human existence:

the stream that preceded the Mystery of Golgotha, and the stream that, following it, will continue for the rest of the earth's existence . . .

Primeval human beings — despite their animal-like organization — were at a higher level than the animal. They possessed an instinctive clairvoyance that enabled them to commune with divine teachers. But like the animal of today they were unconcerned with the approach of death. It never occurred to them, if I may so express it, to pay any particular attention to death. And why? With his instinctive clairvoyance the primeval human being was clearly aware of his true nature even after his descent through birth from the world of spirit into the physical world. He knew that his own essential being had entered into a physical body; and because he could say with certain knowledge that an immortal, eternal being lived within him, the transformation taking place at death was not a matter of interest or concern to him. At most the experience was like that of a snake when it sheds its skin and must replace it with another. The impression of birth and death was taken much more as a matter of course and made far less drastic incision into human existence. People still had a clear vision of the life of the soul.

Today there is no such vision . . . As people began to be ever more aware that death makes a drastic incision not only into earthly physical life but into the life of the soul as well, their attention was inevitably drawn to the fact of birth. Together with this change in human consciousness, earthly life assumed increasing importance since experience of the life of soul was growing dim and people felt themselves more and more removed, during their sojourn on earth, from an existence of soul and spirit. This condition became ever more apparent as the time of the Mystery of Golgotha approached. Among the Greeks it had reached the point where they felt life outside of the physical body to be a shadowy kind of existence, and regarded death as an event fraught with tragedy. The knowledge received by human beings from their earliest divine teachers did not extend to the facts of birth and death ... for birth and death, in the form in which they are experienced on the earth, are experienced *only* on earth and only by human beings. The death of an animal and the dying of a plant are altogether different matters from the death of a human being. And in the divine worlds where the first great teachers of mankind dwelt, there is no birth or death but only transformation, metamorphosis from one state of existence into another. These divine teachers, therefore, had no inner understanding of the experience of dying and being born.

Just think how, in the Old Testament for

example, the mystery of death gradually confronts human beings with an increasing sense of tragedy, and how, in fact, none of the teaching conveyed by the Old Testament gives any adequate or revealing illumination on the subject of death. If, therefore, nothing had happened at the time of the Mystery of Golgotha that differed from what had already happened in the realm of earth, and in the higher worlds connected with the earth, human beings would have faced a terrible situation in their earthly evolution. On the earth they would have lived through the experiences of birth and death which now confronted them not as simple metamorphoses but as drastic transitions in their whole human existence; yet they could have learned nothing of the significance and purpose of death and birth for their earthly life. In order that teachings concerning birth and death might gradually enter humanity it was necessary for the being we call the Christ to enter the realm of earthly life — the Christ who indeed belongs to those worlds from which the ancient teachers had come but who, in accordance with a decision taken in these divine worlds, accepted for himself a destiny different from that of other beings of the divine hierarchies connected with the earth. He lent himself to the divine decree of higher worlds that he should incarnate in an earthly body and with his own divine soul pass through birth and death on earth.[28]

You see, therefore, that what occurred at the Mystery of Golgotha is not merely an internal affair, as it were, of humanity or of the earth, but is equally an affair of the gods. Through the Golgotha event, the gods themselves for the first time acquired inner knowledge of the mystery of death and birth on the earth, for they had previously had no part in either. We have this momentous fact before us: a divine being resolved to pass through human destiny on the earth in order to undergo the same fate, the same experiences in earthly existence, as befall the human being ...

But now ... [Christ] was able to tell [his disciples] what he had experienced and other divine beings had not. From his own divine vantage point he was able to explain to them the mystery of birth and death ... He was able to make clear to them what I will try to express in the following words. They can only be feeble and stumbling because human language has no others to offer.

The human body has gradually become so dense, the death forces in it so powerful that although human beings will now be able to develop their intellect and their own inner freedom they can do this only in a life that definitely experiences death, a life into which death makes a marked

incision, a life from which vision of the immortal soul is
obliterated during waking consciousness. But you can
receive into your souls a certain wisdom. This is the
wisdom which, through the Mystery of Golgotha, my
own being has made possible for you, something with
which you yourselves can be filled if only you can attain
the insight that Christ came down from spheres beyond
the earth to human beings on earth; if only you can come
to realize that here on earth there is something which
cannot be perceived by earthly means but only by means
higher than those of earth; if you can behold the Mystery
of Golgotha as a divine event within earthly life; if you
can apprehend that a God has passed through the Mys-
tery of Golgotha. Through everything else that comes to
fulfilment on earth you can acquire earthly wisdom, but
in order to understand the significance of death to
humanity it would avail you nothing. Earthly wisdom
would suffice only if you, like the people of earlier times,
felt no intense preoccupation with death. But since you
must inevitably be concerned with death, you must
strengthen your perceptive faculty by drawing into it a
force stronger than all earthly forces of perception – a
force so strong that you can realize that in the Mystery of
Golgotha something took place that broke all earthly laws
of nature. If you can include in your beliefs only earthly
laws you will, it is true, be able to observe death, but you
will never discover its significance for human life. But if
you can attain the insight that the earth has now, for the

*first time, received its true meaning and purpose, that at
the midpoint of Earth evolution a divine event has taken
place in the Mystery of Golgotha, an event beyond com-
prehension by means of earthly forms of perception, then
you are preparing a special power of wisdom.*

This power of wisdom is the same as the power of
faith: a special power of spirit wisdom, a faith born
of wisdom. Strength of soul is expressed when a
person can say: 'I believe! I know through faith
what I can never know by earthly means. This is a
stronger force in me than if I only allowed myself to
have knowledge of what can be fathomed merely
by earthly means.' A person is lacking in wisdom,
even if he were to possess all science known on
earth, if his wisdom can only embrace what is
grasped through the laws of nature. To perceive the
reality of the super-earthly within the earthly a far
greater inner activity must be developed ...

This understanding, this insight into the eternal
nature of the human soul, can never be acquired
through brain knowledge, through intellectual
knowledge dependent on the instrument of the
brain ...

During our earthly life the thinking part of the
soul pours itself into the human nervous system,
which it builds up, forms and moulds, and completely inhabits. In the rhythmic system, though, it

is only partially absorbed, giving us some points of reference for further development. But the really eternal element of the human soul is hidden in the metabolic system, in the most earthly and material sphere of our being. Outwardly it is indeed the most material, but because of this very fact the spiritual remains separate from it. The spiritual is drawn into and absorbed by the other parts of the organism, by the brain, and to a lesser extent the rhythmic system, and is no longer independent in those spheres. But it *does* have autonomous existence in the sphere of pure materiality. To use it, however, we would have to develop the ability to see or perceive by means of this materiality. This was a possibility in primeval humanity and although it is not a condition to be striven after it can still occur in pathological states ... ˙

But in the mysteries into which Christ sent his message ... no attempt was made to awaken the old, matter-born knowledge in the manner in which this had been done in primeval humanity, nor the degenerate way subsequently pursued by hashish eaters and others who wished to acquire, through the workings of matter, knowledge not otherwise accessible. But such knowledge was woken instead by clothing the Mystery of Golgotha in ritual, in mantric formulae, above all in the whole structure of the mystery as Revelation,

Offering, Transubstantiation and Communion, in administering the sacrament of the Eucharist in bread and wine. It was not poisons therefore that were offered to the human being here, but the Lord's Supper, clothed in what arises from the mantric formulation of the mass, and from its fourfold membering ... The intention was that after the fourth part of the mass—the Communion—actual communion among the faithful should take place, with the aim of giving at least an inkling that the insights once based upon ancient, metabolic knowledge must be regained.

It is difficult for people today to form any conception of this metabolic-type knowledge, because they have no inkling of how much more a bird knows than a human being—although not in an intellectual, abstract sense—and how much more even a camel, an animal wholly given up to metabolic processes, knows than a human being. It is of course a dim, dreamlike knowledge. What was contained in the metabolic process of primeval man has today reached a degenerate state. But based on the earliest Christian teachings the sacrament at the altar was conceived as a means of pointing to the need to re-acquire a knowledge of the eternal nature of the human soul ...

This knowledge ... ossified in the western Catholic Church, because although the mass was

retained the Church could no longer interpret it ...
But now that mankind has passed through that
period of evolution which shed darkness over the
Mystery of Golgotha, the time has come when
human longings are reaching out for a deeper
knowledge of this Mystery. Such a longing can be
satisfied only through spiritual science, through the
advent of a new knowledge which works in a
spiritual way. The full significance for humanity of
the Mystery of Golgotha will then be acquired once
again. Then people will come to realize that the
most important teachings of all were given not by
the Christ who lived in a physical body until the
Mystery of Golgotha, but by the risen Christ after
the Mystery of Golgotha. People will acquire a new
understanding for words of an initiate such as Paul:
'If Christ be not risen then is your faith vain.' After
the event at Damascus Paul knew that everything
depended upon grasping the reality of the risen
Christ, upon the power of the risen Christ being
united with the human being in such a way that he
can affirm: 'Not I, but Christ in me' ...

Paul knew that if the Mystery of Golgotha had
not taken place, if Christ had not risen, the soul
would be trapped in the destiny of the body, that is
to say, in the dispersion of the elements of the body
into the elements of the earth. Had Christ not risen,
had he not united himself with earthly forces, the

human soul would unite with the body between birth and death, would unite with all the molecules that become part of the earth through cremation or decomposition. By the end of earthly evolution, human souls would eventually have gone the way of earthly matter. But by passing through the Mystery of Golgotha Christ wrests the human soul from this fate. The earth will go her way in the universe, but just as the human soul can emerge from the single human body, so will all human souls be able to free themselves from the earth and go forward to a new cosmic existence. Christ is thus intimately united with earthly existence. But we can only understand this Mystery by approaching it in the way I have described.

To some the question may occur: 'But what of those who cannot believe in Christ?' Let me reassure you. Christ died for all people, for those too who cannot yet unite with him. The Mystery of Golgotha is an objective fact, unaffected by human knowledge. Human knowledge, however, does strengthen the soul's inner forces. All the means at the disposal of human knowledge must therefore be applied so that, in the further course of human evolution, the presence of Christ in this Earth evolution can be a felt and experienced reality, through direct knowledge.

EASTER:
A FESTIVAL FOR THE FUTURE

20. The Grave of Matter

Extract from a lecture given in Berlin on
13 April 1908

Here Steiner emphasizes that the gradual 'loosening' of the etheric from the physical body throughout our further evolution will lead us to a renewed vision of worlds of spirit, but that this may be a fraught experience for those who regard matter as all that matters. Focusing on the 'lost reality' of the physical world such souls will undergo a shattering, deathlike experience, and their spiritual visions will seem like frightening hallucinations. Easter thus points to a far future in which we can gain the capacity to develop spiritual sight, but it is a journey that inevitably passes through the empty grave of the material world.

The whole evolution of mankind has a certain interesting characteristic. It goes forward in one direction until a certain point is reached; then its flow is reversed and it begins to stream back in the opposite direction. Having descended to a certain point, evolution turns upwards again, reaching the same stages as on the descent but now in a higher form. Today we stand before a strange and decisive future. Everyone who is aware of this deeply significant fact of evolution knows that our etheric body[29] will gradually loosen itself again after being submerged in the physical body and after coming to perceive the things of the physical world in their sharply delineated forms. The etheric body must loosen and release itself again so that our being may become spiritualized and have vision once more of the spiritual world. Humanity has actually now reached the point when the etheric bodies of many people are beginning to loosen ...

At what point in humanity's evolution was attainment of full consciousness of the spiritual world made possible for us? It was at the point when Christ set before us the great ideal of humanity by descending into a physical body and then overcoming it. A full understanding of Christ can form the bridge for us between memories of the ancient past and the foreshadowings of the future. When Jesus of Nazareth had reached the age of 30 the Christ descended into his body. Christ was the being who lived once only in a physical body. His victory over death — when rightly understood — shows us how we must live so as to be conscious of the reality of the world of spirit in all future ages. That is the true union with Christ.

How will the Christ mystery live in human beings in the future? ... As we ascend again into the world of spirit we will know that we have gained victory over what we experienced in the physical body; we will look back to the physical as something that has been overcome, surmounted. We should feel the Easter miracle then as a mighty deed, a foreshadowing of the future.

Two possibilities lie before the human being of the future. The one is that he will look back in remembrance to the time of his experiences in the physical body and will say: 'These alone were real. Now I am surrounded by a world of illusion. Life in the physical body — that was the reality.' Such a person will be gazing back upon the physical realm as into a grave, seeing there only a corpse. But the corpse — the physical world — will still represent true reality for him. That is one possibility.

The other is that human beings will look back upon what was experienced in the physical world and will know that it is a grave. Then, with deep awareness of the significance of their words they will tell those who still believe the physical to be the sole reality: 'He whom ye seek is no longer here! The grave is empty and he who lay in it has risen!'

The empty grave and the risen Christ — this is the Easter mystery, which is at the same time a foreshadowing of the future ... This mystery is a deed, a reality inasmuch as we look to Christ not merely as saviour but as the great exemplar and ideal who precedes us and whom we follow, for we too will eventually overcome death ...

In a future by no means far distant the human being will find that the physical world is losing its importance for him. The reality of physical things will already have paled long before humanity's existence on earth has drawn to its close. But when things of the physical world of the senses cease to be all-important and fade into shadow, human beings will either find that the physical is vanishing while they remain incapable of believing in the spiritual realities before them or they will be able to believe and preserve for themselves an awareness of these spiritual realities — and for them there will then be no spiritual death.

To confront a reality that one does not believe in means to be shattered in the spirit. Human beings would be spiritually shattered if, with the loosening of the etheric body, the spiritual worlds were to appear before them without being recognized as such. Many people today could have consciousness of the worlds of spirit but do not, and these worlds therefore rebound upon them. This manifests in restlessness, in nervous conditions, in pathological fears, which are nothing other than the consequences of failure to develop awareness of the spiritual worlds ...

Just as it was our destiny to sink into the deepest depths of material life, so we must be lifted again to knowledge of the spirit. The coming of Christ gave this impulse.

These are the feelings that should inspire us in the days when the symbols of the Easter mystery surround us. For the Easter mystery is not merely a mystery of remembrance but also a mystery of the future, foreshadowing the destiny of those who free themselves increasingly from the shackles, ensnarements and pitfalls of the purely material life.

21. Receiving Christ

Extract from a lecture given in Cologne on
11 April 1909

*In many places the tone of this excerpt, with its beautiful,
rhythmic dialogue of questions and uplifting answers,
resembles a fiery sermon. And one is left with a sense, too,
that the risen Christ is the ultimate answer to the questions embodied in humanity – an answer towards which
we continually evolve. We can only receive Christ,
Steiner says, by growing into his nature ourselves, by
becoming ever more united with one another and so
building the single, universal humanity that Christ
embodies as an ultimate but attainable ideal.*

The Buddha had seen a corpse and had recognized
from it the nothingness of life. People who lived six
hundred years after the event of Golgotha looked
up with fervent devotion to the corpse on the cross.
To them it spoke of life, and in their souls dawned
the certainty that existence is not suffering but leads
across death into blessedness . . . Never was there a
greater reversal in the whole course of human
evolution.

If, six hundred years before our era, entrance into the physical world augured suffering for the human being, how does the great truth that life is suffering present itself to the soul now, after the Mystery of Golgotha? How does it present itself to those who look with understanding at the cross on Golgotha? Does birth, as the Buddha declared, imply suffering? Those who look with understanding at the cross on Golgotha, and feel united it with it, say to themselves: 'Birth, after all, leads us down to an earth which can, from its own elements, provide a raiment for the Christ. We will gladly tread this earth upon which Christ has walked.' Union with Christ kindles in the soul the power to find its way up into the spiritual worlds, brings the knowledge that birth is not suffering but the gateway through which one must pass to find the Redeemer who clothed himself with the very same earthly substances which compose the bodily frame of a human being.

Is illness suffering? No! — so say those who truly understand the impulse of Golgotha — no, illness is not suffering ... For Christ is the great healer of humanity. His power embraces everything that the spiritual can unfold as healing forces, through which illness can be overcome. Illness is not suffering but gives the opportunity to overcome a limitation and a hindrance by unfolding the Christ power within oneself.

Humanity must arrive at a similar understanding of the infirmities of age. The more the feebleness of our limbs increases the more we can grow in spirit, the more we can gain self-mastery through the Christ power indwelling us. Age is not suffering, for with every day that passes we grow into the world of spirit. Death is not suffering either, for it has been conquered in the Resurrection. Death has been conquered through the event of Golgotha.

Can separation from what we love be suffering though? No! Souls permeated with the Christ power know that love can forge links from soul to soul, transcending all material obstacles, links in the spirit that cannot be severed. There is nothing either in the life between birth and death or between death and rebirth to which we cannot spiritually find our way through the Christ impulse. If we permeate ourselves with the Christ impulse, permanent separation from what we love is inconceivable. The Christ leads us to union with what we love.

Equally, to be united with what we do not love cannot be suffering; when we receive the Christ impulse into our souls it teaches us to love all things in their due measure. The Christ impulse shows us the way and, when we find this way, 'to be united with what we do not love' can no longer be suffering; for then there is nothing that we do not encompass with love. Likewise, not attaining what

we yearn for can no longer be suffering if Christ is
with us, for human feelings and desires are so
purified and sublimated through the Christ
impulse that people can yearn only for what is their
due and what is given them. They no longer suffer
because of what they are compelled to renounce; if
they must renounce anything it is for the sake of
purification, and the Christ power enables them to
feel it as such. Therefore renunciation is no longer
suffering ...

As human beings become ever better prepared to
receive the Christ ego or 'I',[30] it will pour in greater
and greater fullness into their souls. They will then
evolve to the level where stood Christ Jesus, their
great exemplar and ideal. Then for the first time
they will come to understand the full extent of
Christ Jesus' great example for humanity. And
having understood this they will begin to realize in
the innermost core of their being that the truth and
assurance of life's eternity springs from the corpse
hanging on the wood of the cross of Golgotha.
Those who are inspired and permeated by the
Christ ego, the Christians of future times, will
understand something else as well, something that
so far has been known only to those who attained
enlightenment. They will understand not only the
Christ who passed through death but also the
triumphant Christ of the Apocalypse, resurrected in

the spiritual fire, the Christ whose coming has been prophesied. The Easter festival can always be for us a symbol of the risen one, a link reaching from Christ on the cross to the triumphant, risen and glorified Christ, to the one who lifts all humanity with him to the right hand of the Father.

And so the Easter festival opens up for us a long vista of the whole future of the earth, of the future evolution of humanity, and is for us a guarantee that those who are Christ-inspired will be transformed from Saul people into Paul people, and will behold with increasing clarity a spiritual fire. Just as the Christ was revealed in advance to Moses and his followers in the material fire of the thorn bush and the lightning on Sinai, so truly he will be revealed to us in a spiritualized fire of the future. *He is with us always, until the end of the world,* and he will appear in the spiritual fire to those who have allowed their eyes to be enlightened through the event of Golgotha. Human beings will behold him in the spiritual fire. They beheld him, to begin with, in a different form; it is in a spiritual fire that they will behold him for the first time in his true form.

But because the Christ penetrated so deeply into earth existence, right into physical bone structure, the power which formed his body out of the elements of the earth purified and hallowed this physical substance. This happened to such a degree

that it can never again become what, in their sor-
row, the eastern sages feared. They feared that in
future the enlightened one, the Maitreya Buddha,
would find no one on earth capable of understanding him because they had sunk so deeply into
matter. Christ was led to Golgotha so that he might
lift matter to spiritual heights once again, so that the
fire might not be extinguished in matter but be
spiritualized ...

A resurrection of the very spirit of the earth itself,
a redemption of humanity, is given us in the symbol
of the Easter bells. This symbol reveals to all who
understand it how the Easter mystery enables us to
climb to spiritual heights. It is not without meaning
that Faust[31] is called back by the Easter bells from
the brink of death to new life, that he is thereby led
to the great moment when he becomes blind before
his death, yet cries: 'But in my inmost spirit all is
light.' Now he can take his further way into the
worlds of spirit where the ennobled elements of
humanity are in safe keeping ...

22. The Message of the Easter Bells

Extract from a lecture given in Cologne on
10 April 1909

Festivals such as Easter enlarge and expand our aware-
ness, and connect us with cosmic realities and great vistas
of time. The Easter bells are a herald of the ultimate
unreality of death.

To begin with we find the world obscure and full of
riddles; we may compare it with a dark room con-
taining many splendid objects which we cannot see
at first. But if we kindle a light the objects in this
room are revealed in all their splendour. Anyone
who strives for wisdom can have such an experience. To begin with we strive in darkness. As we
look into the world, the past and future are veiled in
darkness at first. But when the light that streams
from Golgotha is kindled, everything is illumined,
from the most distant past to the furthest future. For
everything material is born out of the spirit, and out
of matter the spirit will again be resurrected. The
purpose of a festival such as Easter, connected as it

is with cosmic events, is to give expression to this certainty. If human beings are clear, which they can be through spiritual science, that the soul can penetrate the secrets of the universe through such important symbolic festivals as Easter, then they will feel what it means to no longer be confined within a narrow, personal existence, but to live with all that gleams in the stars, shines in the sun and is living reality in the universe. The soul will feel itself enlarged into the universe, becoming more and more filled with spirit.

Resurrection from individual human life to the life of the universe — this is the call that resounds in our hearts from the spiritual bells of Easter. When we hear these bells, all doubt of the reality of the spiritual world will vanish from us and the certainty will dawn that no material death can harm us at all. For we are lifted again into life in the spirit when we understand the message of the spiritual bells of Easter.

The through-cloud shiner:
may he
shine through
light through
glow through
warm through
me too.

Afterword

The last verse of Shelley's poem 'Adonais' — a passionate memorial to his friend Keats — strangely prefigures his own death by drowning while sailing, only one year later at the age of 30. In this last verse he speaks of his 'spirit's bark' (boat) being driven 'far from the shore':

I am born darkly, fearfully afar;
Whilst burning through the inmost veil of
   Heaven
The soul of Adonais, like a star,
Beacons from the abode where the eternal are.

Shelley's early outlook as a firebrand atheist and revolutionary was gradually tempered by personal tragedy. He came to believe that radical social reform would have to be founded on a reform of human moral and imaginative faculties and the redeeming power of love.

In drawing on the myth of Adonis for his tribute to and celebration of Keats, Shelley was tapping into a deep source. In extract 9 in this volume Steiner refers to the story as a pre-Christian myth of resurrection which on the one hand recalled ancient knowledge of the soul's immortality and on the other prefigured the fulfilment of Christ's deed. Describing ancient Adonis celebrations, Steiner relates how an image of the god was immersed in water before returning to life again after three days. All the more startling, then, that Shelley himself drowned in what seemed like such a freak accident. His poem 'Adonais' is itself, in some ways, a journey towards a hard-won Easter experience that passes through a sense of the finality of death ('He will awake no more, oh, never more') to a vision of death overcome. It can thus be seen, in part, as the journey of Shelley's own life—from angry rejection of the institutions of religion to a celebration of inward metamorphosis as opposed to external revolution.

Steiner makes many references to the connection and opposition between spring and autumn, and their presiding festivals. He states that festivals of spiritual resurrection, such as that dedicated to Adonis, were once rightly celebrated in autumn as nature was dying. Shelley seems to have had a particular relationship to autumn, as expressed in perhaps his best-known poem 'Ode to the West Wind', in which he also beautifully links these two seasons as 'sisters' of renewal.

The following three verses from Shelley's 'Adonais' strike me as a fitting conclusion to a volume concerned with resurrection in the widest sense. The god he describes as 'burning through the inmost veil of Heaven' suggests the highest and most selfless, archetypal ego penetrating every layer of existence until all, finally, is illumined. The last verse quoted here is a wonderful invocation of the resurrected god uniting fully with nature and human destiny.

Peace, peace! he is not dead, he doth not sleep—
He hath awakened from the dream of life—
'Tis we, who lost in stormy visions, keep
With phantoms an unprofitable strife,
And in mad trance, strike with our spirit's knife
Invulnerable nothings.—*We* decay
Like corpses in a charnel; fear and grief
Convulse us and consume us day by day,
And cold hopes swarm like worms within our
      living clay.

He has outsoared the shadow of the night;
Envy and calumny and hate and pain,
And that unrest which men miscall delight,
Can touch him not and torture not again;
From the contagion of the world's slow stain
He is secure, and now can never mourn
A heart grown cold, a head grown grey in vain;
Nor when the spirit's self has ceased to burn,
With sparkless ashes load an unlamented urn ...

He is made one with Nature: there is heard
His voice in all her music, from the moan
Of thunder, to the song of night's sweet bird;
He is a presence to be felt and known
In darkness and in light, from herb and stone,
Spreading itself where'er that Power may move
Which has withdrawn his being to its own;
Which wields the world with never wearied love,
Sustains it from beneath, and kindles it above ...

Notes

1. Lucifer and Ahriman are the two polar forces of evil in Steiner's cosmology. Lucifer tempts us away from the earth while Ahriman fetters us to it. Christ is the balancing mediator between these two.
2. As in Paul's very direct, personal experience at Damascus.
3. See also extract 4.
4. Elsewhere Steiner speaks of Easter time as that of 'descent' into earthly life. The apparent contradiction is resolved by understanding that the 'rising' and 'setting' Steiner refers to here are physical in nature, i.e. the flourishing of physical life in spring and its decay in autumn, paralleled by the 'descending' movement of the spirit into earthly life in spring and its ascent from earthly life as physical life wanes in the autumn. See also extract 7.
5. 24 June. See companion volume in this series.
6. See companion volume on Michaelmas.
7. See note 1 above. Ahriman is the name Steiner gives to the entity who seeks to fetter the human being to the earth as a merely animal and material being, denying our spiritual nature.
8. See companion volume in this series.
9. Anthroposophy was the name Steiner gave to his

wide-ranging, Christ-centred philosophy and practice. Literally it means 'wisdom of the human being'.

10. See note 9 above.

11. See companion volume on Christmas. At the Jordan baptism, says Steiner, the divine being Christ united with the body of the human being Jesus.

12. The year was 1913, when the spring equinox (21 March) fell on Good Friday, the spring full moon (22 March) fell on Easter Saturday, and Easter Sunday fell on the next day, 23 March.

13. See note 1 above.

14. The Goetheanum, which Steiner's audience of workmen was building.

15. In Steiner's view we possess, apart from our mineralized physical body, an etheric or life body which we share with the plant kingdom, and an astral or soul body which we have in common with animals. The etheric body is chiefly associated with rhythms, circulation and habitual ways of doing things, while the astral body is the seat of passions, emotions and soul. The fourth and eternal aspect of our being is the 'I' or ego, which continues to exist after death and subsequently seeks reincarnation in a new body.

16. The fact that Mary thought Christ 'was the gardener' also relates to the etheric level which plants and flowers inhabit.

17. That is, non-physical forces of growth and memory. See note 15 above.

18. See, for example, extract 18.

19. See, however, the last paragraph of extract 20.

20. See note 15 above.
21. *Nel mezzo del camin* in Dante's phrase, the 'midpoint of the path'.
22. Karma allows us to evolve by presenting us with situations that belong to us (due to our actions or thoughts in past lives) so that we can try to transform them.
23. Christ is called the 'Son of Man' because he embodies our future evolution and can thus be seen as the further development or offspring of the human race.
24. See note 9 above.
25. See note 1 above.
26. See note 22 above.
27. Cf. John 9:49–52.
28. Cf. Epistle to the Hebrews 2:14–15.
29. See note 15 above.
30. See note 15 above. The Christ ego is humanity's truest, inmost self, towards which it continually evolves.
31. In the play of that name by Goethe.

Sources

Numbers relate to extract numbers in this volume.

1. Dornach, 2 April 1920, in: *The Festivals and Their Meaning*, Rudolf Steiner Press, 2002.
2. Dornach, 3 April 1920, in: *The Festivals and Their Meaning*, Rudolf Steiner Press, 2002.
3. Christiana (Oslo), 21 May 1923, in: *Man's Being, His Destiny and World-Evolution*, Anthroposophic Press, 1984.
4. Dornach, 31 March 1923, in: *The Cycle of the Year*, Anthroposophic Press, 1984.
5. Dornach, 2 April 1923, in: *The Cycle of the Year*, Anthroposophic Press, 1984.
6. Dornach, 21 April 1924, in: *The Easter Festival in the Evolution of the Mysteries*, Anthroposophic Press/ Rudolf Steiner Press, 1988.
7. Dornach, 20 April 1924, in: *The Easter Festival in the Evolution of the Mysteries*, Anthroposophic Press/ Rudolf Steiner Press, 1988.
8. The Hague, 23 March 1913, in: typescript translation, Rudolf Steiner House, London, undated.
9. Dornach, 12 April 1924, in: *From Beetroot to Buddhism*, Rudolf Steiner Press, 1999.
10. Leipzig, 22 February 1916, in: *Life Beyond Death*, Rudolf Steiner Press, 1995.

11. Dornach, 22 April 1924, in: *The Easter Festival in the Evolution of the Mysteries*, Anthroposophic Press/Rudolf Steiner Press, 1988.

12. Munich, 9 January 1912, in: *Esoteric Christianity and the Mission of Christian Rosenkreutz*, Rudolf Steiner Press, 2000.

13. Basel, 1 October 1911, in: *Esoteric Christianity and the Mission of Christian Rosenkreutz*, Rudolf Steiner Press, 2000.

14. Berlin, 12 April 1906, in: *Anthroposophical Quarterly*, vol. 20, issue 1, spring 1975.

15. Dornach, 1 April 1923, in: *The Cycle of the Year*, Anthroposophic Press, 1984.

16. Dornach, 27 March 1921, in: *The Festivals and Their Meaning*, Rudolf Steiner Press, 2002.

17. Berlin, 1 January 1909, in: *The Deed of Christ and the Opposing Spiritual Powers*, Steiner Book Center Inc., 1976.

18. Berlin, 3 April 1917, in: *Building Stones for an Understanding of the Mystery of Golgotha*, Rudolf Steiner Press, 1972.

19. The Hague, 12 April 1912, in: *The Festivals and Their Meaning*, Rudolf Steiner Press, 2002.

20. Berlin, 13 April 1908, in: *The Festivals and Their Meaning*, Rudolf Steiner Press, 2002.

21. Cologne, 11 April 1909, in: *The Festivals and Their Meaning*, Rudolf Steiner Press, 2002.

22. Cologne, 10 April 1909, in: *The Festivals and Their Meaning*, Rudolf Steiner Press, 2002.

Further Reading

Rudolf Steiner's fundamental books:

Knowledge of the Higher Worlds
also published as: *How to Know Higher Worlds*

Occult Science
also published as: *An Outline of Esoteric Science*

Theosophy

The Philosophy of Freedom
also published as:
Intuitive Thinking as a Spiritual Path

Some relevant volumes of Rudolf Steiner's lectures:

Christmas
Michaelmas
St John's
Whitsun

The Four Seasons and the Archangels

For all titles contact Rudolf Steiner Press (UK) or
SteinerBooks (USA):
www.rudolfsteinerpress.com www.steinerbooks.org

Note Regarding Rudolf Steiner's Lectures

The lectures and addresses contained in this volume have been translated from the German, which is based on stenographic and other recorded texts that were in most cases never seen or revised by the lecturer. Hence, due to human errors in hearing and transcription, they may contain mistakes and faulty passages. Every effort has been made to ensure that this is not the case. Some of the lectures were given to audiences more familiar with anthroposophy; these are the so-called 'private' or 'members' lectures. Other lectures, like the written works, were intended for the general public. The difference between these, as Rudolf Steiner indicates in his *Autobiography*, is twofold. On the one hand, the members' lectures take for granted a background in and commitment to anthroposophy; in the public lectures this was not the case. At the same time, the members' lectures address the concerns and dilemmas of the members, while the public work speaks directly out of Steiner's own understanding of universal needs. Nevertheless, as Rudolf Steiner stresses: 'Nothing was ever said that was not solely the result of my direct experience of the growing content of anthroposophy. There was never any question of concessions to the prejudices and preferences of the members. Whoever reads these privately printed lectures can take them to represent anthroposophy in the fullest sense. Thus it was possible without hesitation — when the complaints in this direction became too persistent — to depart from the custom of circulating this material "For members only". But it must be borne in mind that faulty passages do occur in these reports not revised by myself.' Earlier in the same chapter, he states: 'Had I been able to correct them [the private lectures], the restriction *for members only* would have been unnecessary from the beginning.'

The original German editions on which this text is based were published by Rudolf Steiner Verlag, Dornach, Switzerland in the collected edition (*Gesamtausgabe*, 'GA') of Rudolf Steiner's work. All publications are edited by the Rudolf Steiner Nachlassverwaltung (estate), which wholly owns both Rudolf Steiner Verlag and the Rudolf Steiner Archive. The organization relies solely on donations to continue its activity.